Happy cooking!

Miti Ayah

1987

THE FARMER'S COOKBOOK

*A collection of favorite recipes,
economical meal planning methods,
& other tips and pointers from
America's farm kitchens.*

by

Mitzi Ayala

In collaboration with

Carol Rodman

Illustrated by Yoshi Kyhos

CASTLE

For my husband Francisco,
who makes mealtimes magic,
and for my sisters-in-law,
Mary Louise, Marisol, Maria,
Ana Maria, Maria Rosa, and Minako
whose cooking helps cast the spell.

ISBN 0-89009-813-1

Printed in the United States of America.

Arrangement to publish this book has
been made by Castle, a division of
Book Sales, Inc., 110 Enterprise Avenue,
Secaucus, N.J. 07094

The CASTLE trademark is registered in
the U.S. Patent and Trademark Office.

84 85 86 87 3 2 1 9 8 7 6 5 4 3 2 1 0

ACKNOWLEDGEMENTS

To thank Carol Rodman and Evelyn Marquez adequately would take another book. Carol Rodman compiled the recipes, added welcome touches to the text, and is largely responsible for the book's organization. Evelyn Marquez typed the manuscript, and inspired many of the ideas. To say our three-way collaboration has been a happy one is an understatement.

Yoshie Kyhos provided the illustrations, which reflect her imagination, patience, and skill.

Jack Jennings and Bill Alexander from Harbor Publishing served as admired and trusted guides in the preparation of this work.

Peggy Bowes and Michelle Brown joined Carol Rodman and Evelyn Marquez in testing the recipes. Our children, Halsey, Renay, Brandon, Britten, Jose, and Carlos, all joined enthusiastically in the tasting.

California Women for Agriculture deserves an especially hearty thanks. This organization of 5000 women provided information, support—and recipes. Thanks in particular to CWA members Carolyn Leavens and Mike Selbert, who believed in the project; to Leona Lewis and Elsie Bonfantini, who encouraged it; and to Audrey Tennis and Nancy Skinner, who helped spark the original ideas for it.

Thanks also to members of the American Farm Bureau Federation, American Agri-Women, and the Council of California Growers, for their tireless help and advice.

Thanks most of all to American agriculture, the quiet giant that contributes more to our nation's balance of payments than any other export. It was American agriculture that inspired this book.

CONTENTS

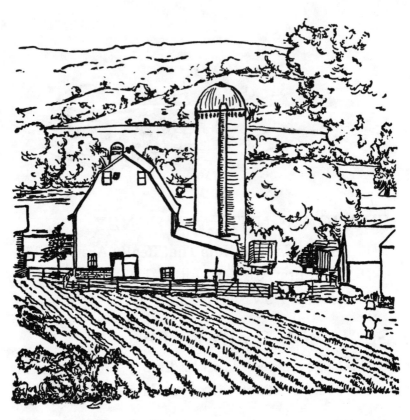

Introduction

Suppose for a moment that *you* come from a rice-growing family. Having all the rice you could use, you'd probably try out hundreds of rice recipes in the course of the years. You'd also swap recipes with other rice-growing friends, and at get-togethers with them, you'd probably talk a lot about how to store, cook, and serve rice. More than likely, you'd also have a few special rice recipes handed down from your mother-in-law and perhaps from your own grandmother too. Whenever you read a newspaper or magazine or county extension pamphlet that mentioned rice, you'd automatically pay attention and read on.

The fact is, few people in the world—except other rice growers—would probably know as much about cooking with rice as you. And wouldn't the same thing hold true if you grew tomatoes or peaches or beef?

The Farmer's Cookbook is based on the premise that the men and women who grow any crop know best how to cook with it. In *The Farmer's Cookbook*, you'll find tips from such experts on buying, handling, storing, preparing, and above all appreciating the fresh foods they grow.

A tomato grower, for example, will tell why you should never refrigerate a tomato. (The delicate tissues of this tropical plant will deteriorate rapidly at temperatures below 50 degrees Fahrenheit.) A bean farmer will tell you how to cook beans so you'll never suffer from...er... windiness. (Soak beans for twenty-four hours to leach out the gas-causing oligosaccharides, throw out the soak water, and *then* cook.) Strawberry farmers will explain why strawberries shouldn't be washed until just before they're eaten. (Washing dissolves the strawberry's natural waxy coating and allows water to enter it as it would a sponge. A rapid breakdown of vitamin C and loss of flavor result.)

Each chapter highlights a specific food. Along with the tips we've just mentioned, you'll find anecdotes about the product, nutritional information, and scrumptious, tried-and-true farmers' recipes. And, remembering our own dilemma—"How will we use *all* those peaches that have ripened at once?"—we offer a menu built around a generous use of each highlighted food. You'll be surprised to see how versatile a single fresh food can be. Just for example, rice can appear in your menu all the way from soup to dessert!

Farmers surely don't have all day to cook. The recipes you'll find here, then, emphasize the happy combination of a short preparation time and use of the fresh, unprocessed foods that are generally available in neighborhood supermarkets. Don't expect to find yourself searching in out-of-the-way markets for expensive and exotic ingredients for these recipes; nor should you be opening many cans! *The Farmer's Cookbook* should become the first book you reach for when you need a fresh, wholesome, and above all tasty dish.

Enjoy!

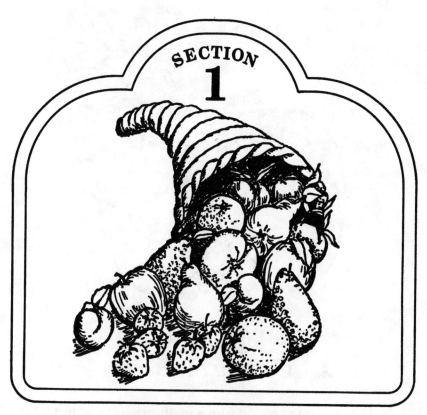

SECTION
1

FRUITS

1 | APPLES
Getting the Best

Next time you're biting into a fresh, crisp apple, think for a moment about where it came from. In fact, don't stop there but imagine that it's spring, the bees have finished pollinating the apple blossoms, and you're standing in the middle of an orchard in front of a typical apple tree— about twelve feet tall—and you've got a task ahead of you. About 1600 baby apples are growing on that tree. If you don't thin three-quarters of them, not only will you get small, unmarketable fruits, but also the tree will be so thoroughly exhausted that it will hardly bear at all the following year.

You look up at the tree. The apples are so thick on the

branches they almost look like grapes. And you've got to knock off 1200 of them!

Farm Advisor Dick Bethel is looking over your shoulder. "Try to thin them so there's only one every six or eight inches," he suggests, and then adds sympathetically, "It's a time-consuming job, but when you're an apple grower, and you know you're only going to get one paycheck a year, you have a tendency to develop a lot of patience."

You begin picking off the surplus apples, and soon the ground is covered with them. In three to five hours you're done.

If you were an experienced thinner, one who had developed speed and skill like a fast typist, you could have finished the job in an hour. But remember, in all this time of working, you've only thinned one tree. Now put yourself in apple-grower Cal Able's shoes. A modern orchard might contain two hundred trees to the acre, and Cal has twenty acres to look after. If 1200 apples are to be thinned from each tree, then Cal is faced with thinning nearly *half a billion* apples each spring.

In the past, orchards contained far fewer trees to the acre. Seventy used to be a pretty standard number a couple of decades ago, but in today's orchards trees are planted close together to trap as much of the sun's energy as possible. The apple tree is actually a living solar collector, and if the trees are planted close together, fewer of the sun's rays reach the ground, wasted. There's an ecological advantage to this new way of doing things: weed control is simplified if the tree is catching most of the sunlight.

After all this work goes into making good-sized, healthy apples, how do we select good ones in the supermarket? Many growers would counter this question with an invitation to us to buy the apples directly from them, and have a picnic in apple country at the same time.

But for those of us who can't make the trip, here are some tips. "Buy bagged apples," suggests farmer's wife

Norma Brubaker. "These are usually smaller than the ones out on display, but they're just as tasty, they're perfect for small kids' lunches, and they're a lot less expensive. And best of all, they haven't been handled." She goes on to recommend that we choose an apple by eyeballing it rather than touching it. "Look for a bright color and unblemished skin. Touching it is going to leave bruise marks, those little fingerprint marks . . . I know you've seen them. The grocer is going to have to throw out bruised fruit and every time this happens, it brings the prices up."

What's the sweetest apple? Farm Advisor Bethel points out that apples are all pretty similar in sugar content if they're at the same stage of ripeness. "But," he emphasizes, "this does not mean they're all going to taste equally sweet. The acidity of an apple controls how sweet it's going to taste." According to Bethel, the Red Delicious, being low in acids, will taste sweetest, followed by Golden Delicious. Stayman Winesap and Jonathan will taste quite tart, while a pippin has an intermediate taste.

If you want a real treat, try making your own fresh apple sauce. Just peel, core, and coarsely chop some apples. Simmer in a covered saucepan with a small amount of water for twenty minutes or so, or until the apples are soft. Then, either mash or put them through a food mill and add a few drops of lemon juice and maybe a little brown sugar.

Nutritionally, apples are a winner. They're a good source of needed potassium and vitamin A, have almost no fat, and are an excellent, low-calorie snack food. Just keep them well-chilled in the vegetable crisper of your refrigerator and they'll keep for several weeks.

Apples
in the Menu

Weekend Brunch

Applejack   Hot Spiced Cider

Fresh Fruit and Cheese Cubes

Eggaroni**

Giant Apple Pancake*

Apple Buttermilk Bran Muffins*

Moist Apple Bread*

Coffee   Tea

*See Apple Recipes
**See Egg Recipes

Apple Buttermilk Bran Muffins

Batter:

This recipe makes about one-half gallon of batter, which gets better as it gets older.

½ cup (4 fl. oz.) butter
1 cup (7 oz.) sugar
¼ teaspoon salt
2 eggs
2½ teaspoons baking soda
2 cups (16 fl. oz.) buttermilk
2½ cups (13 oz.) all-purpose flour
1½ cups (4 oz.) all-bran or bran buds

In a bowl, cream together butter, sugar, salt, and eggs. In a large bowl, combine baking soda and buttermilk. Alternating in thirds, add the flour, bran, and buttermilk mixture to the creamed mixture. Storable for up to six weeks in a tightly covered, nonmetal container.

Muffins:

3 cups (24 fl. oz.) batter
1 cup (6 oz.) apples, finely chopped

Preheat oven to 400° F. (205° C.).
Stir together batter and apples. Pour mixture into greased muffin pans and bake for 15 to 20 minutes.

Moist Apple Bread

⅓ cup (2½ fl. oz.) butter
⅔ cup (4½ oz.) sugar
2 eggs, beaten
2 cups (10 oz.) all-purpose flour
1 teaspoon baking powder
1 teaspoon baking soda
½ teaspoon salt
1½ cups (12 oz.) coarse apple sauce
1 tablespoon lemon juice
¾ cup (3 oz.) walnuts, chopped

Preheat oven to 350° F. (180° C.).

Cream butter and add sugar until mixture is light and fluffy. Beat in eggs. Sift together flour, baking powder, baking soda, and salt. Add flour mixture alternately with apple sauce to egg mixture. Stir in lemon juice and nuts. Bake in a greased and floured 9 by 5 inch (23 by 13 cm.) loaf pan for 50 to 60 minutes.

Apple Celery Salad

2½ cups (15 oz.) Red and Golden Delicious apples, unpeeled and diced
1 tablespoon lemon juice
1 tablespoon sugar
pinch of salt
1 cup (6 oz.) celery, chopped
½ cup (2 oz.) walnuts, chopped

Toss apples with lemon juice. Add sugar, salt, celery, and nuts and toss well to combine. Chill.

Giant Apple Pancake

3 tablespoons butter
4 eggs
1 cup (8 fl. oz.) milk
1 cup (5 oz.) all-purpose flour
1 tablespoon sugar
½ teaspoon salt
3 tablespoons butter
3 apples, peeled, cored, and sliced
3 tablespoons light-brown sugar
1 tablespoon lemon juice
1 tablespoon brandy or 1 teaspoon vanilla
1 cup (8 fl. oz.) sour cream
1 tablespoon sugar
¼ teaspoon cinnamon
⅛ teaspoon nutmeg

Preheat oven to 425° F. (220° C.).

Place 3 tablespoons butter in a heavy oven-proof, 10-inch (25-cm.) or 12-inch (30-cm.) skillet. Melt butter in oven.

Meanwhile, place eggs and milk in blender and blend until combined. Add flour, sugar, and salt and blend on high for 1 minute. Pour into hot skillet over melted butter. Bake for 20 minutes. Pancake will be very puffy.

While pancake cooks, melt 3 tablespoons butter in a saucepan and sauté apple slices and brown sugar until apples are translucent. Add lemon juice and brandy or vanilla and boil to reduce liquid. Keep warm.

Beat together sour cream, sugar, cinnamon, and nutmeg.

To serve, spread apple mixture over hot pancake and cut in wedges. Garnish with sour cream mixture.

Apple and Pork Loin Roast

3 to 5 pounds pork loin
salt and pepper, to taste
thyme or sage, to taste
6 Rome Beauty apples, cored, with top half pared
½ cup (3½ oz.) sugar
½ teaspoon cinnamon
6 tablespoons (3 fl. oz.) butter

Preheat oven to 325° F. (165° C.).

Place the pork in a shallow baking pan. Season with salt, pepper, and thyme or sage. Roast, allowing 35 minutes per pound, until a meat thermometer shows the pork to be 170° F. (77° C.). Remove from oven approximately 45 minutes before cooking is completed.

Place the apples around pork. Combine sugar and cinnamon, pour into each apple cavity. Place 1 tablespoon butter on each apple. Return pork to oven and bake for remaining 45 minutes.

Cider Apple Crisp

3 pounds apples (about 9 medium apples)
½ cup (4 fl. oz.) apple cider
1 cup (5 oz.) flour, white or whole wheat
1 cup (7 oz.) brown sugar
½ cup (4 fl. oz.) butter
1 teaspoon cinnamon

Preheat oven to 350° F. (180° C.).

Peel, core, and slice apples into an 8 by 8 inch (20 by 20 cm.) pan. Pour cider over them. Mix together flour, brown sugar, butter, and cinnamon to make a crumbly pastry. Sprinkle mixture over apples and bake for 40 minutes.

Georgia Apple Bars

2 cups (13½ oz.) sugar
1 cup (8 fl. oz.) vegetable oil
juice of half a fresh lemon
2 teaspoons vanilla
2 eggs, beaten
3 cups (15 oz.) all-purpose flour
1¼ teaspoons baking soda
1 teaspoon salt
3 cups (18 oz.) apples, peeled and chopped
1 cup (4 oz.) walnuts, chopped
1 cup (7 oz.) brown sugar
½ cup (4 fl. oz.) butter
¼ cup (2 fl. oz.) milk
2 teaspoons vanilla

Preheat oven to 325° F. (165° C.).

In a bowl, mix together sugar, oil, lemon juice, vanilla, and eggs. Stir together flour, baking soda, and salt, and add to sugar mixture. Fold in apples and nuts. Bake in greased and floured 9 by 13 inch (23 cm. by 33 cm.) pan for 1½ hours.

Combine brown sugar, butter, milk, and vanilla in a saucepan and boil for 7 to 10 minutes, or until almost crystallized. Pour topping over cool cake. Allow cake to stand overnight before serving.

New England Apple Sauce Loaf Cake

This moist, dark loaf cake is delicious alone or topped with a cream cheese frosting. Tastes even better the second day.

1½ cups (12 fl. oz.) fresh apple sauce
½ cup (4 fl. oz.) butter
1 cup (7 oz.) sugar
1 cup (5 oz.) raisins
1 teaspoon nutmeg
1 teaspoon ground cloves
1 teaspoon cinnamon
½ teaspoon salt
2 teaspoons baking soda
2 cups (10 oz.) all-purpose flour
½ cup (2 oz.) walnuts, chopped

Preheat oven to 350° F. (180° C.).

In a saucepan, combine apple sauce, butter, sugar, and raisins. Heat mixture until butter melts. Allow to cool. Sift together nutmeg, cloves, cinnamon, salt, baking soda, and flour. Stir flour mixture into apple sauce mixture. Add nuts. Pour batter into a greased 9 by 5 inch (23 by 13 cm.) loaf pan and bake for 1 hour.

2 | APRICOTS
*The Beauty
and Fitness Fruit*

You have to be alert if you want to buy fresh apricots. The problem is that while supermarkets generally need a two-week lead time to place their newspaper advertising, apricot growers know only one week in advance when their crop will be ready for harvesting.

Since the season in any one area lasts only two or, at most, three weeks, many supermarkets never do manage to advertise fresh apricots. "If you're relying on newspaper ads," cautions Stan Tufts, a third-generation apricot grower, "you may find the 'cot' season is over before you knew it started."

If you are lucky enough to find fresh apricots in your local supermarket, how can you select good ones? "Avoid shriveled or mushy-looking ones," says grower Jack Hestilow. "Apricots with a yellowish-orange or golden color are ready for immediate eating, but if your market happens to have only ones tinged with green, you can buy them anyway and count on them ripening in a few days at home. If the greenish ones have any color at all, they already have sufficient sugar content to ripen into very good fruit."

The process can be speeded by putting the apricots in a ripening bowl, or if you don't have one, Hestilow suggests "the old original ripening bowl—a brown paper bag."

Once ripe, the apricots can be held for three or four days in the refrigerator. "Put them in a plastic bag or the vegetable crisper," advises grower Eddie Tufts. "You want to make sure they won't dry out," she adds.

Eddie has some other advice. "Some of the new apricot varieties have great eye-appeal. But don't overlook the smaller, less colorful older varieties. They are extremely tasty and juicy."

Besides tasting delicious, apricots are a nutritional bargain. Each apricot contains only 18 calories, but provides approximately 1000 International Units of vitamin A, or 20 percent of the Recommended Daily Allowance.

Vitamin A is sometimes referred to as the beauty vitamin, since it is important for maintaining healthy skin and glowing hair. It is also essential for growth and maintenance of body tissue, strong bones and teeth, and good eyesight.

Athletes and those 55 million Americans who exercise daily are discovering that apricots are an energy food, too. Most of the nation's 16.5 million joggers are probably looking for the elusive wonder food that will help them improve their performance. Apricots can't claim that title, of course, but they do meet a lot of joggers'—and any other sportspeople's— requirements for vitamin C and iron. The apricot's winning ingredient, however, is potassium, a mineral needed by the muscles to release heat during exercise. You can be sure that apricots are popular among marathoners before the big race!

Apricots
in the Menu

DINNER PARTY

Apricot Creams*   Apricot Brandy Alexander*

Cheese and Crackers

California Pinot Chardonnay

Chilled Apricot Salad*

Shrimp Scampi*

Hot Buttered Rice

Stir-Fry Zucchini and Carrots**

Bavarian Apricot Torte*

Coffee or Tea   Brandy

*See Apricot Recipes
**See Honey Recipes

Apricot Creams

12 apricots
½ cup (4 fl. oz.) sour cream
¼ cup (1 oz.) walnuts, chopped

Halve apricots and remove pits. In a cup, blend sour cream and walnuts. Spoon mixture into apricot hollows. Chill until serving time.

Apricot Brandy Alexander

2 cups (16 oz.) apricots, chopped
1 cup (8 fl. oz.) heavy cream or 1 cup (8 oz.) vanilla ice cream
6 tablespoons (3 fl. oz.) crème de cacao
1 cup (8 fl. oz.) milk
6 tablespoons (3 fl. oz.) brandy

Place apricots, cream or ice cream, crème de cacao, milk, and brandy into a blender. Blend until smooth. Pour into chilled glasses.

Chilled Apricot Salad

1 cup (8 oz.) apricots, quartered and pitted
1 cup (8 oz.) pineapple chunks
2 oranges, peeled and cut into bite-size pieces
2 cups (16 fl. oz.) sour cream

Combine apricots, pineapple, oranges, and sour cream, and gently stir to blend thoroughly. Cover and chill for at least 24 hours. To serve, spoon salad into sherbet glasses or chilled lettuce cups.

Apricot Sunshine Breakfast Cake

¾ cup (5 oz.) sugar
1 egg
¼ cup (2 fl. oz.) soft shortening
½ cup (4 fl. oz.) milk
1½ cups (9½ oz.) all-purpose flour
2 teaspoons baking powder
½ teaspoon salt
2 tablespoons butter
½ cup (3½ oz.) brown sugar
8 apricots, halved and pitted
8 walnuts, halved

Preheat oven to 375° F. (190° C.).

Mix sugar, egg, and shortening thoroughly. Stir in milk. Blend in flour, baking powder, and salt. Melt butter and pour into an 8 by 8 inch (20 by 20 cm.) pan. Sprinkle brown sugar over the melted butter. Place apricots cut side down in rows of 4. Spread cake mixture over apricots and bake for 25 to 35 minutes. When cake is done, invert it onto a plate and place a walnut half in each apricot cup. Serve warm.

Shrimp Scampi

¼ cup (2 fl. oz.) butter
2 pounds large shrimp, shelled and deveined
2 garlic cloves, minced
4 cups (32 oz.) apricots, halved and pitted
⅓ cup (1 oz.) parsley, chopped
2 tablespoons lemon juice
¾ teaspoon salt
¼ teaspoon pepper

In a large frying pan, melt butter. Add shrimp and garlic and sauté for 3 to 5 minutes, until shrimp turns pink. Stir in apricots, parsley, lemon juice, salt and pepper. Cook for 2 to 3 minutes, until apricots are warm. Serve immediately.

Oven–Barbecued Chicken Wings

2 cups (16 oz.) apricots, pitted and chopped
2 tablespoons catsup
2 tablespoons vegetable oil
1 tablespoon lemon juice
½ teaspoon salt
3 pounds chicken wings

Preheat oven to 425° F. (220° C.).

Combine apricots, catsup, oil, lemon juice, and salt in a blender. Blend until smooth. Place chicken wings on a rack in a shallow baking pan. Brush with sauce. Bake 30 minutes, basting with sauce every 10 to 15 minutes. Serve extra sauce with chicken.

Yogurt Fruit Salad

2 cups (16 oz.) apricots, pitted and halved
2 apples, cored and cut into wedges
1 cup (6 oz.) seedless grapes
¼ cup (1 oz.) pecans
½ cup (4 fl. oz.) plain yogurt

Combine apricots, apples, grapes, and pecans. Add yogurt and stir gently to mix well. Chill.

Grandma's Pickled Apricots

This elegant accompaniment to meat and poultry makes a wonderful gift.

7 pounds whole apricots, approximately 7 dozen
  apricots
whole cloves, as needed
⅓ ounce stick cinnamon
1 pint (16 fl. oz.) vinegar
4 pounds sugar, white, brown, or mixed
brandy, as needed (optional)

Wash apricots and stick two or three cloves into each one. Combine cinnamon sticks, vinegar, and sugar in a large pan and bring to a boil. Add half the apricots and boil gently until soft. Repeat, using remaining apricots. Pack fruit into hot sterilized jars, adding enough hot cooking liquid to cover fruit. Add a piece of cinnamon stick and 1 tablespoon brandy, if used, to each jar. Seal at once.

Bavarian Apricot Torte

Shell:

> ½ cup (4 fl. oz.) butter
> 3 tablespoons sugar
> 1 cup (5 oz.) all-purpose flour

Preheat oven to 450° F. (230° C.).

Cream together butter and sugar; stir in flour until smooth. With fingertips, spread dough in an even layer to line the bottom and sides of a 9-inch (23-cm.) pan with removable bottom. Bake for 10 minutes. Remove from oven.

Filling:

> ⅓ cup (3 oz.) cream cheese
> ¼ cup (1¾ oz.) sugar
> ¼ teaspoon lemon peel, grated
> 1 egg
> 3 cups (24 oz.) apricots, halved and pitted
> ¼ cup (1 oz.) almonds, sliced
> 3 tablespoons sugar
> ½ teaspoon cinnamon

Cream together cream cheese, ¼ cup (1¾ oz.) sugar, and lemon peel; add egg and mix well. Pour mixture into pastry shell. Arrange apricots over cheese mixture; sprinkle almonds on top. Combine 3 tablespoons sugar and cinnamon; sprinkle over top. Bake in 450° F. (230° C.) oven for 10 minutes. Reduce heat to 400° F. (205° C.); continue baking for 25 minutes longer. Cool before removing sides of pan; then chill thoroughly.

Apricot Cobbler

12 to 14 apricots, halved and pitted
1 cup (5 oz.) all-purpose flour
1 cup (7 oz.) sugar
¼ cup (2 fl. oz.) butter
1 egg, beaten
½ teaspoon salt
2 teaspoons baking powder
1 cup (8 fl. oz.) heavy cream, whipped

Preheat oven to 350° F. (180° C.).

Place apricots in a well-buttered 8 by 8 inch (20 by 20 cm.) oven-proof pan. Combine flour, sugar, butter, egg, salt, and baking powder. Mix until thoroughly combined. Sprinkle mixture over apricots and bake for 30 minutes. Serve with whipped cream.

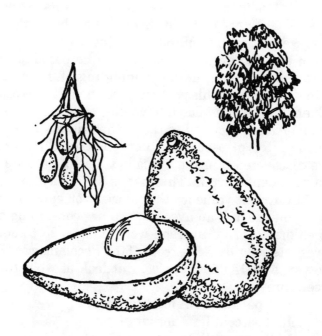

3 | AVOCADOS
The Love Fruit

In 1519, when Hernando Cortez entered Mexico, he discovered undreamed of wealth in gold and jewels, an amazingly complex administrative system, and—a new fruit, the avocado. Cortez and his soldiers have, among their many distinctions, that of being the first white men to savor an avocado.

If *you* have yet to eat an avocado, consider this description by Oviedo, a companion of Cortez: "In the center of the fruit is a seed like a peeled chestnut. And between this and the rind is the part which is eaten, which is abundant, and is a paste similar to butter and of a very good taste."

Cortez and his followers had an additional reason for

being enthusiastic about the fruit besides its "very good taste." The Aztecs had told them of their belief that avocados were a strong aphrodisiac. Modern research has a way of proving ancient medicines to be based on truth, but to the avocado growers' abiding regret, research has yet to substantiate this particular claim for the avocado.

Even if avocados don't have the love properties the ancient Aztecs ascribed to them, the growers have other reasons to be pleased with them. Nutrition researchers have discovered that the avocado is one of nature's most "nutrient dense" fruits. This means that an avocado gives a lot of nutrient value for the calories you eat. For example, if you eat half an avocado, you are consuming about 138 calories; for an average woman, ages 23 to 50, this represents roughly 6.8 percent of the Recommended Daily Allowance (RDA) for calories. But look at what this 6.8 percent provides:

> 12.5 percent RDA for vitamin A
> 15.3 percent RDA for vitamin C
> 16.8 percent RDA for vitamin E
> 12.5 percent RDA for folic acid
> 8.0 percent RDA for riboflavin
> 8.2 percent RDA for thiamine
> 9.0 percent RDA for pyridoxine
> 10.8 percent RDA for niacin

An avocado is really a bargain in terms of calories versus nutrients.

How do you select a good avocado? Angelo Granaroli, an avocado grower, says the best plan by far is to buy your avocados while they're still hard, three or four days before you want to use them. Let them ripen at room temperature out of the sunlight for three or four days, until they're just slightly soft.

You can hurry this process along somewhat by putting the avocados in a brown paper bag or by wrapping them in foil. This speeds ripening by concentrating the fruit's own ethylene gas, which is the factor that causes ripening. Once the fruit is ripe, it can be stored in the refrigerator for up to ten days.

Why not simply buy ripe avocados on the day you need them? Granaroli answers: "They'll still be good, but the soft ones you find in the supermarket may have been squeezed by many shoppers and thus bruised into ripeness rather than naturally ripened."

If Granaroli had his way, no one would squeeze an avocado in the store, but instead would select a firm one and buy it.

Betty Brown, another avocado grower, gives this hint for selecting good avocados. "If a store avocado feels rubbery, like a hard rubber ball, don't buy it. The avocado was picked before it was fully mature, and the oil content—which is what gives an avocado its delicious flavor—is not what it should be." Avocados contain at least 8 percent oil, but, emphasizes Betty Brown, "that's the cholesterol-free kind."

Carolyn Leavens, President of California Women for Agriculture, has an additional tip for us. "Don't refrigerate an avocado before it's finished ripening. It will never ripen further once it's been chilled."

*Avocados
in the Menu*

SUPPER PARTY

Chilled Wine   Beer

Guacamole Grande*

Tortilla Chips

California Pinot Blanc

Del Mar Molded Salad*

Crusty French Rolls and Butter

San Clemente Curry*

Rice

Chutney

Artichoke Nut Chiffon Cake**

Coffee or Tea

*See Avocado Recipes
**See Artichoke Recipes

San Juan Cocktail

¼ cup (2 oz.) tomato, diced
2 tablespoons green onions, sliced
2 tablespoons celery, diced
⅛ teaspoon salt
7 ounces minced clams, with liquid
¼ cup (2 oz.) catsup
2 tablespoons lemon juice
dash Tabasco sauce
¼ teaspoon Worcestershire sauce
¼ teaspoon prepared horseradish
1 avocado

In a bowl, combine tomato, onions, celery, salt, clams and liquid, catsup, lemon juice, Tobasco sauce, Worcestershire sauce, and horseradish. Chill mixture thoroughly. When ready to serve, peel and dice avocado and add to mixture. Toss well. Spoon into cocktail glasses.

Guacamole Grande

2 avocados
1 onion, finely chopped
1 jalapeño pepper, peeled, seeded, and chopped
1 tomato, chopped and drained
salt and pepper, to taste
2 teaspoons salad oil
tortilla chips, as needed

Halve avocados, peel, and remove pits. Smash pulp in bowl with a fork. Add onion, pepper, tomato, salt, and pepper. Stir in just enough salad oil to moisten. Cover bowl with plastic wrap and chill.
Serve with tortilla chips.

Very Easy Gazpacho

4 to 5 small tomatoes, peeled
¼ cup (2 fl. oz.) olive oil
½ teaspoon basil
1½ teaspoons herb salt or to taste
½ teaspoon lemon juice
¼ teaspoon marjoram
1 cucumber, chopped
1 green pepper, chopped
1 tomato, chopped
1 avocado, diced

Place peeled tomatoes, olive oil, basil, herb salt, lemon juice, and marjoram in a blender. Blend until combined. Add cucumber, green pepper, chopped tomato, and avocado to tomato mixture. Chill for several hours before serving.

Chilled Fallbrook Soup

2 avocados
½ cup (4 fl. oz.) sour cream
4 small tomatoes, peeled and finely chopped
1¼ cups (10 fl. oz.) beef stock
¼ cup (1½ oz.) green onions, finely chopped
1 teaspoon salt or to taste
1 or 2 tablespoons lemon juice
dash Tabasco sauce

Halve avocados. Remove seeds and skin. Blend avocados or push through a sieve and mix with sour cream. Stir in tomatoes, beef stock, green onions, salt, lemon juice, and Tabasco sauce. Chill.

Del Mar Molded Salad

2 or 3 avocados
3 tablespoons lemon juice
1¾ teaspoons salt
⅛ teaspoon Tabasco sauce
1½ envelopes plain gelatin
½ cup (4 fl. oz.) cold water
1 cup (8 fl. oz.) boiling water
1 cup (8 fl. oz.) sour cream
1 cup (8 fl. oz.) mayonnaise
¼ cup (1½ oz.) green onions, sliced
1 large tomato, diced
salad greens, as needed

Cut avocados in half; peel, mash, and sieve or blend until smooth. Add lemon juice, salt, and Tabasco sauce. Soften gelatin in ½ cup (4 fl. oz.) cold water; then dissolve in boiling water and cool to room temperature. Stir in avocado mixture, sour cream, and mayonnaise; chill until mixture mounds on spoon. Fold in onions and tomato; turn into a 5-cup (40-oz.) ring mold and chill until firm. Unmold and garnish with salad greens.

Can be served with tostadas.

Avocado and Shrimp Salad

1 avocado, peeled and diced
1 tomato, diced
1 bunch green onions, including tops, chopped
8 ounces fresh shrimp, shelled and deveined
juice of ½ lemon
salt and pepper, to taste
lettuce leaves, as needed

Mix together avocado, tomato, green onions, and shrimp. Add lemon juice, salt, and pepper. Best if made the night before or early on the day of serving.

To serve, mound mixture onto lettuce leaves.

San Clemente Curry

4 tablespoons butter
12 ounces fresh shrimp, shelled and deveined
1½ teaspoons curry powder
1¼ teaspoons salt
1 medium tomato, chopped
1 medium onion, chopped
2 tablespoons lime or lemon juice
1 cup (8 fl. oz.) sour cream
3 avocados

Melt three tablespoons butter in a saucepan and sauté shrimp until pink. Set aside.

Melt remaining butter in a saucepan. Add curry powder and salt and cook 1 minute. Add tomato and onion; cook until soft. Add lime or lemon juice, shrimp, and sour cream. Heat thoroughly, but do not allow to boil. Halve avocados, skin, and remove seeds, and fill centers with curry mixture.

Can be served with rice and chutney.

Avocado Caesar Salad

1 tablespoon butter
⅛ teaspoon garlic powder
1½ cups (6 oz.) small bread cubes
½ cup (4 fl. oz.) vegetable oil
¼ cup (2 fl. oz.) lemon juice
½ teaspoon Worcestershire sauce
⅛ teaspoon dry mustard
¼ teaspoon pepper
¼ cup (1 oz.) grated Parmesan cheese, or more, to
  taste
¾ ounce anchovy fillets, drained and chopped
2 quarts torn lettuce (Romaine or iceberg)
1 egg
1 avocado

In a saucepan, heat butter and garlic powder; sauté bread cubes in mixture until golden. Remove from heat. In a salad bowl, combine oil, lemon juice, Worcestershire sauce, mustard, pepper, and Parmesan cheese. Add anchovies and lettuce; toss. Break egg onto salad and toss until flecks of yolk disappear. Peel and dice avocado and add to salad. Toss in prepared bread cubes.

4 | ORANGES
Their Beauty Is More Than Skin Deep

The next time you sit down to your breakfast orange juice, ask yourself what you might possibly have in common with monkeys, guinea pigs, and bats. The answer? If you add a few exotic birds, you will have the entire list of creatures that need vitamin C and cannot make it inside their own bodies.

Fortunately for the select few of Nature's creatures who need vitamin C, oranges are a particularly delightful source. A single orange will meet all a person's Recommended Daily Allowance for vitamin C, and will provide small amounts of other vitamins, minerals, natural sugars, water, and cellulose besides. And it will taste delicious!

Don't be confused by the different varieties of oranges. Basically, two kinds are most often available—Valencias, the most popular oranges in the world, and navels, introduced into the United States relatively recently. Navel oranges—the winter oranges—are usually used for eating, in contrast to Valencias, which are primarily juice oranges. Navels are easy to peel, fall naturally into sections, and, as an added gift, are totally seedless. You can easily recognize them in your supermarket because they alone have the characteristic navel at one end. Look for them from November through May.

Next time you're in your favorite market, take a look at the small mountain of navel oranges. Every navel orange you'll see there, and every navel orange in every store or stand in the entire world, traces its ancestry to one branch of a particular tree in remote Bahia, Brazil. Just over a hundred years ago, a Brazilian citrus farmer noticed that a branch of one of his trees was heavy with fruits much larger than those on neighboring branches. Curious, he ate one of the fruits and discovered an orange-colored goldmine. That chance mutation in the branch of his tree had yielded an entirely seedless orange blessed with an exquisite tangy flavor.

Twelve cuttings from that Brazilian tree were sent to this country, where they were grafted onto our rootstocks. From those cuttings has sprung the entire navel orange industry.

The navels, by the way, will always be orange. But when isn't an orange orange?

Ask ruggedly handsome Jack Heeger of Sunkist Growers, Incorporated, and he'll happily explain that Valencia oranges, the variety of orange you can buy from late February through November, can be at the peak of their flavor and still be green. And to confuse matters, they can also be quite acidic—that is, have very little sugar—and still be a perfect orange color. "With Valencia oranges," Jack insists, "color doesn't mean anything. A Valencia may turn just the right golden orange color in winter before it's fully mature, but as the weather turns warmer, it will actually start to turn green again, beginning at the stem end."

Such an orange is going through a process referred to in the industry as "regreening." The chlorophyll inside the fruit migrates out to the surface of the fruit, tinging the skin with green. "One of the things that we at Sunkist would most like the public to hear about, and that few know about right now, is that the greenish color on the Valencia in the supermarket is an indication that the fruit is ripe."

To get the most juice from a Valencia, bring it up to room temperature, and then roll it on the counter a few times to break down the juice sacs. If you have half an orange left over after filling your juice glasses, you can refrigerate it in a plastic bag or wrap it for later use with only minimal loss of vitamin C. In citrus, vitamin C is uniquely stable because of a substance that inhibits the usual oxidation of vitamin C. This is the same substance that does the job when you squeeze lemon juice on avocados, apples, or bananas to keep them from discoloring. Fortunately for us, who are dependent on a daily intake of vitamin C for our health, very little vitamin C is lost during shipping, marketing, home storage, or common preparations for eating.

When you're selecting oranges, what should you look for? The fruit should feel firm and heavy, never spongy, and should be free of blemishes or soft spots. Oranges will keep at room temperature for about two weeks, and refrigerated in the covered vegetable crisper (where they should be kept, for humidity, if refrigerated), they will last up to a month and a half.

Oranges not only make a handy, nutritious snack, but also they have a detergent action that cleans teeth and stimulates the gums as well. And, to quote food authority Mary Louise Lau, "A good, sweet, ripe orange is one of the most sensual experiences that can happen to the human palate."

*Oranges
in the Menu*

BRUNCH

Freshly Squeezed Orange Juice   Orange Gin Fizzes

Western Orange-Egg Scramble*

Hot Buttered English Muffins

Something Special Orange Coffee Cake*

Yogurt Fruit Salad**

Freshly Ground Coffee   Tea

*See Orange Recipes
**See Apricot Recipes

Orange Nut Bread

Peel:

   3 oranges
   1 cup (7 oz.) sugar
   2 tablespoons water

Peel the oranges and cut the peel into strips. Boil in salted water until tender. Drain. Add sugar and water and boil until liquid is clear, about 1 minute. Allow to cool.

Batter:

   2 eggs
   1 cup (7 oz.) sugar
   1 cup (8 fl. oz.) milk
   ¼ teaspoon salt
   4 cups (20 oz.) all-purpose flour
   1 tablespoon baking powder
   ¾ cup (3 oz.) walnuts or pecans, chopped

Preheat oven to 350° F. (180° C.).

Beat eggs until frothy. Add sugar and beat until creamy. Add milk and salt and mix well. Sift together flour and baking powder and fold into egg batter. Add nuts, prepared peel, and syrup. Spread mixture evenly in two greased and wax-paper-lined 9 by 5 inch (23 by 13 cm.) loaf pans. Bake for 30 to 45 minutes.

Good served plain or with cheese spreads or peanut butter.

Something Special Orange Coffee Cake

Cake:

1 cup (8 fl. oz.) butter
2 cups (13½ oz.) sugar
4 eggs
3½ cups (16¼ oz.) all-purpose flour
1 teaspoon baking soda
1 cup (8 fl. oz.) buttermilk
2 cups (8 oz.) walnuts, chopped
1 cup (4 oz.) coconut, flaked
1 pound oranges, sliced
½ pound dates, pitted and chopped

Preheat oven to 275° F. (135° C.).

Cream together butter and sugar. Add eggs one at a time and beat well. Sift together flour and baking soda. Add to butter mixture in thirds, alternating with buttermilk. Stir in walnuts, coconut, oranges, and dates. Mix well. Pour into a 9 by 13 inch (23 by 33 cm.) pan and bake for 45 or 50 minutes, or until done. Cool in pan.

Topping:

2 cups (13½ oz.) powdered sugar
1 cup (8 fl. oz.) orange juice

To prepare topping, combine powdered sugar and orange juice. Beat well. Pour over cooled cake.

Breakfast on the Run

4 English muffins
4 slices (about 4 oz.) mild cheese
2 oranges, peeled and sliced in thick
   cartwheels
4 slices (about 6 oz.) cooked ham
¼ cup (2 oz.) orange marmalade

Split muffins; place on baking sheet. On 4 muffin halves, arrange cheese, orange cartwheels, and ham. Brush top of ham and remaining 4 muffins halves with marmalade. Broil 6 inches from heat for 5 to 7 minutes until heated through. Press muffin halves together.

Hungryman's Grilled Sandwich

¼ cup (2 fl. oz.) butter, softened
2 teaspoons orange peel, grated
8 slices whole wheat bread
8 slices (about 8 oz.) mild cheese
2 oranges, peeled and sliced in cartwheels
1 avocado, peeled and sliced

In a small bowl, combine butter and orange peel. Lightly spread both sides of bread slices with butter mixture. Assemble 4 sandwiches with layers of cheese slices, orange cartwheels, and avocado slices. In a large skillet, cook sandwiches on both sides until bread is lightly browned and cheese starts to melt.

Three-Generation Salad

3 oranges, peeled and sliced in half-
  cartwheels
3 avocados, peeled and sliced
1 cup (8 fl. oz.) catsup
1 cup (8 fl. oz.) vegetable oil
½ cup (4 fl. oz.) cider vinegar
1 teaspoon salt
½ teaspoon garlic salt
dash pepper
¼ cup (1¾ oz.) sugar, or more to taste

Arrange orange and avocado slices in an alternating pattern on a platter. In a blender, mix thoroughly the catsup, oil, vinegar, salts, pepper, and sugar. Pour mixture over fruit and serve.

Western Orange-Egg Scramble

8 eggs, slightly beaten
⅓ cup (3 oz.) cream cheese, cubed
2 tablespoons milk
peel of half an orange, grated
¼ teaspoon dried dill weed
dash salt and pepper
2 tablespoons butter
2 oranges, peeled and cut into bite-size pieces

In a bowl, combine eggs, cream cheese, milk, orange peel, dill, salt, and pepper. In a large skillet, melt butter; add egg mixture. Stirring occasionally, cook over medium-low heat until eggs are almost set. Add orange pieces; continue cooking until eggs are set but still moist.

Skillet Orange Chicken

2 tablespoons butter
2½ pounds chicken, in serving-size pieces
1 tablespoon orange peel, grated
½ cup (4 fl. oz.) orange juice
1 onion, chopped
2 tablespoons honey
2 tablespoons water
1½ tablespoons all-purpose flour
1 orange, peeled and sliced in half-cartwheels

Melt butter in a large skillet. Add chicken and cook for 15 minutes, or until well browned. Add orange peel, orange juice, onion, and honey. Cover and cook over low heat for 30 minutes. Remove chicken to a serving dish. Gradually blend water into flour, then pour into juices in skillet. Cook, stirring, until mixture thickens. Add orange slices.

To serve, pour sauce over chicken.

Sherried Orange Dessert

8 navel oranges
1½ cups (6 oz.) sweetened coconut, grated
¾ cup (6 fl. oz.) sherry

Peel and slice oranges into cart-wheel slices ¼ inch (¾ cm.) thick. In a glass bowl, arrange slices and coconut in alternating layers, ending with a layer of coconut. Pour sherry over all, and chill for at least an hour.

Orange Meringue Pie

Filling:

 2 cups (13½ oz.) sugar
 ¼ teaspoon salt
 1½ tablespoons orange peel, grated
 5 tablespoons cornstarch
 2 cups (16 fl. oz.) orange juice
 3 egg yolks
 2 tablespoons butter
 2 tablespoons lemon juice
 1 teaspoon lemon peel, grated
 1 9-inch (23-cm.) pie shell, baked and cooled

Mix together sugar, salt, and orange peel. Combine cornstarch with a little of the orange juice and mix until a smooth paste is formed. Add remaining orange juice, the sugar mixture, egg yolks, butter, lemon juice, and lemon peel. Pour into a double boiler and cook, stirring, until mixture thickens. Remove from heat and allow to cool. Pour into pie shell.

Meringue:

 3 egg whites
 6 tablespoons powdered sugar
 powdered sugar, as needed

Preheat oven to 325° F. (165° C.)
Beat egg whites until thick. Slowly add powdered sugar and continue to beat until stiff peaks form. Mound meringue over filling and bake pie for 10 minutes, or until meringue browns lightly.

To serve, dust lightly with powdered sugar if desired.

Orange Ice

1 cup (7 oz.) sugar
2 cups (16 fl. oz.) boiling water
1 envelope unflavored gelatin
1 tablespoon cold water
2 cups (16 fl. oz.) orange juice, strained
4 tablespoons lemon juice, strained

Combine sugar and boiling water, stirring until sugar dissolves. Boil for 5 minutes. Soften gelatin in cold water; add to sugar mixture. Add orange juice and lemon juice. Pour into freezer trays and place in freezer. Stir occasionally until almost frozen. Remove nearly frozen ice from freezer, place in a bowl, beat well with an egg beater. Return mixture to freezer trays and freeze.

5 | PEACHES
Antiquity's "Persian Apple"

As long ago as the Fifth Century B.C., the ancient Chinese wrote about *tao,* the peach, considering it a symbol of immortality. Traveling westward with the caravans into Asia Minor, the peach became abundant in Persian gardens, where it achieved fame as the "Persian apple." Later, Spanish explorers carried this fruit to Europe and the New World, where today one-fourth of the world's supply of peaches is produced.

Pound for pound, fresh peaches are less expensive than most snacks, crackers, cookies, chips, or candies. Furthermore, peaches are the most economical of the summer fruits, often selling for bargain prices at the peak season, the end of July and beginning of August. Packed with nutrients, full of flavor, and low in calories—only 40 in a medium-size peach—these fruits are penny- and pound-wise, too.

A peach provides a quarter of the Recommended Daily Allowance of vitamin A and 10 percent of the recommended vitamin C. Also, minerals, fiber, and B vitamins are present in significant amounts.

Peaches can be classified in two major and quite distinct categories: clingstone and freestone. A freestone peach differs from a clingstone, and not just because its pit comes free easily. "Anyone could tell the difference blind-folded," says Gertie Zehrung, a clingstone grower. "The flesh of a freestone is soft, something like a ripe pear. The clingstone is crisper, like an apple. And the flavors are completely different."

The freestone is generally for fresh use rather than for canning. It's what you'll see in the supermarkets most often.

The peaches found in the supermarkets happen to be a somewhat sensitive issue among the peach growers. Gertie Zehrung and her friend Ruby Bergman, a freestone peach grower, puzzle over the quality of peaches they see in the supermarkets. "I wonder why we never see the best quality there," says a quizzical Gertie. Ruby shakes her head, adding, "The supermarkets never show just how great a peach can be. What you see there is often what I'd call seconds . . . or thirds."

John Starn, from the California Freestone Peach Association, has an answer to the mystery that puzzles the two women and many others in their industry. "Growers," he explains, "want to show off their best, ripe fruit, and consumers love it. But in between, there are handlers, brokers, distributors, and retailers. These in-between groups have trouble accepting the best ripe fruit."

Starn goes on to explain that there is a logic to the position of the middlemen. "If you were a broker, and two growers came to you, one with perfectly ripe fruit that has to be moved immediately, and the other with slightly green fruit that you knew would keep for several weeks, which would you be inclined to buy? Remember, you can't hold on to the ripe fruit and bargain until you get a good price; you must sell to whomever will take it. Otherwise, it's going to spoil, and you've lost your money. On top of that, you know your competition is going to buy the fruit that will keep longer, providing them with more money and fewer headaches."

How do you pick a good peach? John Starn says, "The bright, rosy blush on the cheeks of a fresh peach is lovely to look at—but don't be deluded. 'Red' does not mean 'ripe,' and blushes differ from one variety to the next." The red look, he goes on to explain, has eye appeal, but it isn't necessarily associated with flavor. "If I were looking for a good peach, I'd look for one that looked full and plump at the stem end, not wrinkled. I'd look for a deep and uniform yellow or creamy background color with no trace of green. And I'd avoid hard-looking fruits. I don't want a fruit that looks like I could play baseball with it."

At home, store fresh ripe peaches in the refrigerator. They'll stay fresh for a few days. Unripened peaches will ripen up nicely in a loosely closed bag. For a scrumptious peachy taste, serve them at room temperature.

Did you ever wonder why a peach is so thirst-quenching on a hot summer day? That's because it's nearly 90 percent water and has very little sodium and no additives or preservatives. Surely, the lovely, exotic peach is good for you!

*Peaches
in the Menu*

SUMMER LUNCH

Fresh Peach Fizz*

Champagne

Chilled Fallbrook Soup**

The Peachiest Chicken Salad*

Warm Rolls and Butter

Fresh Peach Cobbler*

Coffee or Tea

*See Peach Recipes
**See Avocado Recipes

Fresh Peach Fizz

2 peaches, peeled and sliced
1 tablespoon lemon juice
2 tablespoons sugar
½ teaspoon orange-flower water
1 egg white
¼ cup (2 fl. oz.) gin
1 cup (6 oz.) ice, crushed
sparkling water, as needed

Place peaches, lemon juice, sugar, orange-flower water, egg white, gin, and ice in a blender container. Cover and blend until smooth. Fill tall glasses ¾ full. Pour sparkling water into glasses. Serve with long-handled spoons and straws.

Peach Freeze

People paid fifty cents a glass for this delicious beverage at a California Women for Agriculture fundraiser. Many said it was so good it should have sold for seventy-five cents.

3 cups (1½ lb.) peaches, peeled and sliced
1½ cups (12 oz.) vanilla ice cream
3 cups (18 oz.) ice, crushed

Whirl peaches, ice cream, and ice in blender until creamy smooth. Serve in chilled glasses.

Loafer's Peachy French Toast

8 slices white or whole wheat bread
1 pound Monterey Jack or other mild cheese, cut
    in ¼-inch (¾-cm.) slices
4 eggs
1 cup (8 fl. oz.) half-and-half
½ teaspoon salt
⅛ teaspoon pepper
3 cups (1½ lb.) peaches, peeled and sliced
powdered sugar, to taste

Preheat oven to 425° F. (220° C).
    In a well-buttered 9 by 5 inch (23 by 13 cm.) glass loaf
pan, arrange a layer of bread slices. Top with a layer of
cheese. Repeat layers, ending with bread. Beat eggs. Stir
in half-and-half, salt, and pepper. Pour egg mixture over
cheese and bread. Bake for 25 to 30 minutes or until puffy
and golden brown. Cool in pan 10 to 15 minutes. Loosen
edges, invert onto serving platter, and surround with
peaches. Sprinkle with powdered sugar. Slice and serve.

Pick-Up Peach Salads

This recipe makes a tasty appetizer or "finger salad" that
you can pick up to eat.

6 peaches
juice of 1 lemon
⅔ cup (6 oz.) cream cheese, softened
½ cup (4 fl. oz.) sour cream
¼ cup (1 oz.) almonds, chopped
¼ cup (2 oz.) dates, chopped
2 tablespoons crystallized ginger, chopped
fresh mint sprigs, as needed

Halve and pit peaches but do not peel. Sprinkle fruit with lemon juice to keep it from darkening. Chill. Meanwhile, in a small bowl, combine cream cheese, sour cream, almonds, dates and ginger. Spoon mixture into peach halves. Arrange on serving tray. Garnish with mint sprigs. Serve with napkins.

The Peachiest Chicken Salad

6 peaches
2 tablespoons lemon juice
3 cups (24 oz.) chicken, cooked and chopped
½ cup (3 oz.) celery, sliced
⅓ cup (1½ oz.) sunflower seeds
4 to 6 tablespoons mayonnaise
½ teaspoon salt
dash pepper
⅔ cup (6 oz.) cream cheese, softened
3 tablespoons chutney
3 tablespoons coconut, toasted
6 lettuce leaves
6 slices Swiss cheese
cucumber slices

Peel peaches by immersing them in boiling water for about 30 seconds. With a slotted spoon, transfer peaches to cold water. Slip off skins. Brush with lemon juice. Chill.

Prepare chicken salad by mixing chicken, celery, sunflower seeds, mayonnaise, salt and pepper. Chill.

At serving time, mash half the cream cheese with chutney and half with coconut. Shape six balls of each. Halve peaches, remove pits, and place creamed mixture in peach cavities. For each serving, on lettuce-lined salad plates, arrange two peach halves on a nest of chicken salad (about ½ per cup per person). Add a slice of cheese and some cucumber slices to each plate.

Peachy Ham Slice

1 ham slice
3 tablespoons butter
1 cup (8 fl. oz.) water
½ cup (3½ oz.) sugar
4 tablespoons currant jelly
2 tablespoons lemon juice
1½ teaspoons grated lemon peel
4 peaches

Gently sauté ham in butter.

In a saucepan, combine water, sugar, jelly, lemon juice, and lemon peel. Cover and simmer for 5 minutes. Peel, halve and pit peaches and place cut side down in sauce. Cover and simmer for 10 minutes. Turn and cook 5 more minutes.

To serve, place ham on platter and garnish with peaches and sauce.

Fresh Peach Cobbler

¼ cup (2 fl. oz.) butter
1 cup (7 oz.) sugar
1 egg, beaten
3 peaches, peeled and chopped
1 cup (5 oz.) all-purpose flour
1 teaspoon baking soda
½ teaspoon nutmeg
½ teaspoon cinnamon
pinch salt
½ cup (2 oz.) walnuts
1 cup (8 fl. oz.) heavy cream, whipped

Preheat oven to 325° F. (165° C.).

Cream butter and sugar. Add egg and beat well. Add peaches. Sift together flour, baking soda, nutmeg, cinnamon, and salt. Stir into peach mixture.

Pour batter into buttered 9-inch (23 cm.) square pan. Sprinkle nuts on top. Bake for 35 to 40 minutes.

Serve with whipped cream.

Molded Peaches and Cream Dessert

1 envelope unflavored gelatin
¾ cup (5 oz.) sugar
3 or 4 freestone peaches, peeled
½ teaspoon vanilla
⅛ teaspoon almond extract
2 egg whites
1 cup (8 fl. oz.) heavy cream
peach slices, as needed

In a saucepan, stir together gelatin and sugar. Puree peaches in blender (should yield about 1¾ cups), and stir into gelatin mixture. Heat, stirring well, until gelatin and sugar are completely dissolved and mixture just reaches a boil. Remove from heat and stir in vanilla and almond extract. Set pan in ice water and stir until mixture is almost set.

In a bowl, combine egg whites and heavy cream. Beat until stiff peaks form. Gently stir gelatin mixture and fold it into cream mixture. Pour into a 1-quart mold, cover, and chill for at least 4 or 5 hours, or until set.

Serve garnished with peach slices.

Peach Cake

1 cup (8 fl. oz.) shortening
1¼ cups (8½ oz.) sugar
2 eggs
1 teaspoon vanilla
2 cups (16 oz.) peaches, mashed
1 cup (5 oz.) raisins
2 cups (10 oz.) all-purpose flour
½ teaspoon salt
1 teaspoon allspice
1 teaspoon cloves
1 teaspoon cinnamon
1½ teaspoons baking soda
1½ teaspoons cocoa

Preheat oven to 350° F. (180° C.).

In a mixing bowl, cream shortening and sugar. Add eggs, one at a time, and beat well. Add vanilla. In a saucepan, heat peaches and raisins until raisins are plumped; cool slightly and add to creamed mixture.

Sift together flour, salt, allspice, cloves, cinnamon, baking soda, and cocoa. Carefully stir into peach mixture. Pour into a greased 13 by 8 inch (33 by 20 cm.) pan. Bake for 30 to 45 minutes.

Serve plain, or garnished with whipped cream and sliced peaches.

6 | PEARS
The Great Golden Fruit

Some secretaries type with machine-gun speed. Some newspaper stuffers insert supplements so fast their work looks like a continuous stream. A skilled pianist moves his fingers over the keyboard so rapidly you have no idea where he's touched.

The pears you buy in the supermarket also involve a mind-boggling skill, and a visit to the Pear Fair in Courtland, California, will convince you of this. The annual Pear Packers Contest determines the fastest pear packers from the various packing sheds. Contestants are judged on the speed with which they pack two boxes of 120 pears each. A recent winner, Doratha Wiseman, loaded a lug in just one second more than two minutes. That's a pear a second, perfectly positioned.

If you're in a competitive mood, you could also match your pear-peeling ability against Fern Cummings. Recently she won the pear-peeling contest by making a continuous pear peel measuring 78¼ inches. The contest rules allow you ten minutes for making the peel.

The Pear Fair is just a sample of how much the pear growers enjoy their own fruit. "Pears are so versatile," exclaims Marilyn van Loben Sels, wife of a grower. "I make pear pie, pear Waldorf salad, pear sauce. In fact, any recipe that works for apples works for pears."

If she's going to substitute them for apples, Marilyn likes her pears green, the way you buy them in the supermarket. Although some people like pears on the greenish side, while they're still crisp and tart, most prefer their pears to be a sunny golden yellow.

Why, then, are pears so often sold green in the supermarket? "Because," answers Mark Faye, a grower, "pears are one of the few fruits that don't ripen well on the tree. If you leave them on the tree until ripe, you'll find them both mushy and grainy. We've discovered that the optimum development of flavor and texture comes when we pick them green and allow them to ripen off the tree."

If you're hungry for pears and want to eat them soon, select those approaching a yellow color and that yield to gentle pressure—but don't pinch, please. Pinching causes brown spots that will make the fruit unmarketable.

To ripen pears at home, leave them at room temperature for several days. As the starch in them is converted to sugar, a subtle sweet flavor will develop and the buttery, juicy flesh will soften. The skin will change its color at the same time, signaling the changes inside.

To ripen them faster, put them either in a ripening bowl or a loosely closed paper bag. Inside, the fruits' own natural ethylene gas, which is the chemical mechanism that causes the fruit to ripen, will become concentrated.

Ripe pears should be stored in the refrigerator to prevent them from becoming over-ripe too fast. On the other hand, to keep green pears from ripening, you can hold them for weeks and sometimes months in your refrigerator's vegetable crisper.

When you're ready to eat them, put your pears in the refrigerator for a short time. Pears are best eaten when slightly chilled.

What about pears and nutrition? A medium-size pear contains only about 100 calories, but has a significant amount not only of B vitamins, vitamin C, and minerals, but also nearly half of the 6 grams of fiber recommended for adults each day. Containing over 80 percent water, pears are natural thirst-quenchers and offer a healthful alternative to other snack products on the market.

❧   ❧

Pears
in the Menu

DINNER

California Zinfandel

Bacon-Pear-Avocado Salad*

Rolls and Butter

Glazed Meatballs with Pears*

Egg Noodles

Kentucky Fried Corn**

Pear Crumble Pie*

Coffee or Tea

*See Pear Recipes
**See Corn Recipes

❧   ❧

Pear Nut Bread

2 eggs, beaten
1 cup (5 oz.) whole bran
¼ cup (1 oz.) coconut, grated
1¼ cups (10 oz.) pears, peeled, cored, and finely
    chopped
1½ cups (7½ oz.) all-purpose flour
½ cup (3½ oz.) brown sugar
1 teaspoon baking powder
½ teaspoon salt
½ teaspoon baking soda
¼ cup (2 fl. oz.) butter, softened
½ cup (2 oz.) walnuts, chopped

Preheat oven to 350° F. (180° C.).

Combine eggs, bran, and coconut. Stir in pears. Allow to stand a few minutes. Mix together flour, brown sugar, baking powder, salt, and baking soda. Add butter and bran mixture. Mix well. Stir in walnuts. Pour batter into a greased 9 by 5 inch (23 by 13 cm.) loaf pan and allow to stand for 20 minutes. Bake for 1 to 1¼ hours. Allow to stand 10 minutes. Turn bread out of pan and cool on a rack. Excellent toasted.

Bacon-Pear-Avocado Salad

½ pound bacon
1 head iceberg lettuce, chilled
2 avocados, peeled and cubed
3 pears, peeled, cored, and cubed
1 tablespoon lemon juice

In a pan, fry bacon until crisp. Drain and crumble. Line salad plates with lettuce. Toss together avocado cubes, pear cubes, and lemon juice. Place on lettuce. Sprinkle bacon over and serve immediately.

Crunchy Pear Salad

¼ cup (2 fl. oz.) lemon juice
3 tablespoons vegetable oil
2 tablespoons honey
2 tablespoons peanut butter (optional)
1 teaspoon orange peel, grated
¼ teaspoon salt
¼ teaspoon onion salt
dash dry mustard
dash curry powder
6 pears, peeled, cored, and halved
½ cup (2 oz.) peanuts, finely chopped
2 oranges, peeled and sliced
lettuce leaves, as needed

Combine lemon juice, oil, honey, peanut butter (if used), orange peel, salts, mustard, and curry powder. Beat ingredients together until well blended. Turn into a shallow dish, and roll pears first in dressing, then in chopped peanuts. On each of six plates, arrange two pear halves and two orange slices on lettuce leaves. Spoon remaining dressing over all.

Almond Pears and Chicken

1 teaspoon salt
¼ teaspoon white pepper
1 teaspoon paprika
½ teaspoon powdered ginger
3 pounds frying chicken, in serving-size pieces
¼ cup (2 fl. oz.) vegetable oil
⅓ cup (2⅔ fl. oz.) sauterne
⅓ cup (2⅔ fl. oz.) orange juice
2 or 3 pears
⅓ cup (1⅓ oz.) almonds, slivered and toasted

Combine the salt, pepper, paprika, and ginger. Season chicken with the mixture. Brown chicken slowly on both sides in heated oil. Add wine and orange juice. Cover and cook until chicken is almost tender, about 20 minutes. Peel, core, and halve pears. Add fruit to pan, basting with some of the liquid. Continue cooking, covered, until chicken and pears are tender, about 10 minutes longer. Remove to a heated serving platter. Skim and discard any excess fat from pan liquid. Bring to a full boil and pour over chicken. Sprinkle with almonds.

Glazed Meatballs with Pears

1 pound lean ground beef
½ cup (4 oz.) onion, finely chopped
¼ cup (1¼ oz.) raisins, finely chopped
¼ cup (1 oz.) parsley, finely chopped
¼ cup (1 oz.) Parmesan cheese, grated
1 thick slice bread
1¼ cups (10½ fl. oz.) beef stock
1 large egg, beaten
1¼ teaspoons seasoned salt
¼ teaspoon pepper
dash garlic powder
2 tablespoons vegetable oil
1 tablespoon cornstarch
1 tablespoon lemon juice
1 teaspoon sugar
1 teaspoon paprika
1 small bay leaf
4 large pears

Combine beef, onion, raisins, parsley, and Parmesan cheese. Soften bread in ½ cup (4 fl. oz.) stock (reserve remainder for sauce). Combine softened bread with meat mixture, egg, salt, pepper, and garlic powder; mix well. Shape meat into 12 to 16 balls. Heat oil in a large skillet and brown meatballs; remove from pan. Stir cornstarch into pan drippings. Measure remaining stock and add water to make 1½ cups (12 fl. oz.). Add to skillet, along with lemon juice, sugar, paprika, and bay leaf. Heat to boiling, stirring. Return meatballs to skillet. Cut each pear in half, lengthwise. Remove peel and core, and cut fruit into thick slices. Add to pan and simmer, basting frequently, until meatballs are cooked through and pears are tender.

Bartlett Pot Roast

2 tablespoons all-purpose flour
2 teaspoons onion powder
1 teaspoon salt
¼ teaspoon pepper
3 to 4 pound chuck roast
2 tablespoons vegetable oil
4 whole cloves
2 inches (5 cm.) stick cinnamon
½ cup (4 fl. oz.) dry red wine
3 to 4 pears, peeled, cored, and quartered
1 tablespoon red wine vinegar

Combine flour, onion powder, salt, and pepper. Rub mixture into surface of meat. In a Dutch oven, heat oil and slowly brown meat on all sides. Add cloves, cinnamon, and wine. Cover tightly and simmer for about 2½ hours or until tender. Add more wine if necessary. Transfer roast to heated serving platter. Pour off excess fat. Add pears and vinegar; cover and cook 10 to 15 minutes. Arrange pears around roast. Strain gravy and serve in a gravy boat.

Pear-Raspberry Leather

This delicious leather may not last long enough to store away. Although it is easy to make in a food dehydrator, you may also dry it in the sun.

1 cup (5 oz.) raspberries*
2 tablespoons lemon juice
pears, as needed, peeled, cored, and quartered

Into a quart-size blender container, place raspberries, lemon juice, and as many pears as needed to make a quart of puree. Blend until smooth. Spread puree onto dehydrator trays covered with plastic wrap, using a spatula to form a rectangle approximately 9 by 13 inches (23 by 33 cm.). Dry puree for 8 to 14 hours, or until the leather will pull away from the plastic wrap. After it dries, peel leather away from plastic, roll lengthwise, and cut into 3-inch-wide strips. Tightly wrap the leather in plastic to store.

*You may omit raspberries, increasing the amount of pears and adding cinnamon and ginger to the puree.

California Pears Helene

1 cup (6 oz.) semi-sweet chocolate chips
¼ cup (3 fl. oz.) honey
½ cup (4 fl. oz.) half-and-half
3 fresh pears, peeled, cored, and halved
6 scoops vanilla ice cream

In a saucepan over low heat, melt chocolate chips with honey. Add half-and-half and stir until well blended.

To serve, place pear halves round side down in a dessert bowl. Fill hollow with ice cream and top with chocolate sauce.

Pear Crumble Pie

Pastry:

> 1½ cups (7½ oz.) all-purpose flour
> 1½ teaspoons sugar
> 1 teaspoon salt
> ½ cup (4 fl. oz.) vegetable oil
> 2 teaspoons milk

Sift together flour, sugar, and salt in a 9-inch (23-cm.) pie plate. With a fork, whip together oil and milk and pour over flour mixture. Mix with fork until all flour is dampened (it will form a ball in center of plate). Press dough evenly against bottom and sides of pie plate. Crimp edges.

Filling:

> 3 tablespoons sugar
> 3 tablespoons cornstarch
> dash salt
> 1 teaspoon lemon peel
> 3 tablespoons lemon juice
> 6 to 8 pears, peeled, cored, and thinly sliced
> ½ cup (4 fl. oz.) butter
> ½ cup (3½ oz.) brown sugar
> ½ teaspoon cinnamon
> ½ teaspoon ginger
> 1 cup (5 oz.) all-purpose flour

Preheat oven to 425° F. (220° C.).

Combine sugar, cornstarch, salt, lemon peel, and lemon juice. Toss with pears and arrange in pie shell. Mix butter, brown sugar, cinnamon, ginger, and flour until crumbly. Sprinkle over top of pears.

Bake for 45 to 50 minutes.

Sour Cream Pear Pie

1 9-inch (23-cm.) pie shell, unbaked
5 or 6 pears, peeled, cored, and thinly sliced
4 tablespoons all-purpose flour
⅔ cup (4½ oz.) sugar
¼ teaspoon ginger
¼ teaspoon nutmeg
1 cup (8 fl. oz.) sour cream
1 tablespoon sugar
½ teaspoon nutmeg

Preheat oven to 425° F. (220° C.).

In pie shell, arrange pears in concentric circles with stem end toward center. Combine flour, ⅔ cup (4½ oz.) sugar, ginger, ¼ teaspoon nutmeg, and sour cream. Mix well and pour over pears. Combine 1 tablespoon sugar and ½ teaspoon nutmeg and spread over pie. Bake 35 to 40 minutes.

7 | STRAWBERRIES
Luscious and Lovely

"Doubtless God could have made a better berry, but doubtless God never did."

Strawberry growers love to echo this old saying because it happens to refer to their fruit. If you taste fresh strawberries (they're on the market from mid-March through November), you may be inclined to agree with these farmers. Low in calories, high in nutrients, and luscious in flavor, strawberries are a genuine treat.

But there is a catch. To get the full benefit of these berries, you have to select good ones and store them correctly. Dave Riggs, of the California Strawberry Advisory Board, has some suggestions on how to do just that.

"First, select fully ripened, bright red strawberries,"

Riggs advises. Unlike many fruits, strawberries do not ripen after being picked. The whitish ones stay white.

Riggs suggests that once you have brought them home, you use them soon to make sure you receive the most delectable flavor and the highest nutritional value. To keep them before use, remove the berries from their containers, arrange them—without washing them or taking off their stems—in a single layer on a cookie sheet or other shallow container, and place them in the refrigerator. Treated this way, the berries should keep fresh and attractive for several days.

Sherry Mehl, wife of a strawberry grower, says that the thing consumers most need to know about strawberries is: don't wash them until *just* before using them. "Washing," she explains, "breaks down a protective outer layer and the berry just won't last as long without it. The fruit will lose its sheen and quickly get dried out and crinkly." When you are ready to wash the berries, put them in a large strainer and rinse them gently in cool water. Pat them dry with a towel, then—if your recipe directs—carefully remove the caps by using the point of a sharp knife or giving them a twist.

Remember to leave the stems *on* while washing. Removing the stem allows water to soak into the strawberry, diluting the flavor, washing away some of the vitamin C, and changing the texture.

Before serving the berries, allow time for them to reach room temperature. As Dave Riggs explains, "Various flavor factors which are locked in at refrigerator temperatures are released at room temperature. If you wait until they've gradually warmed up, you won't have to sugar them so much."

Unsugared, strawberries are a tremendous nutritional bargain. A full cup of whole strawberries contains only 60 calories, and that 60 calories provides 150 percent of the daily vitamin C requirement. Strawberries are also high in fiber and contain significant amounts of iron.

Strawberries are scrumptious *au naturel* with the caps still attached for dipping into powdered sugar, sour cream, thick unflavored yogurt—or even chocolate sauce.

How does a farmer's wife recommend using strawberries? Sherry Mehl says, "If you want a really healthy breakfast, serve your favorite cold cereal topped with sliced fresh strawberries and low-fat milk. You'll be getting protein, bulk, vitamins, carbohydrate, loads of flavor—and it won't make you fat."

*Strawberries
in the Menu*

DESSERT PARTY

Champagne

Peach Freezes**   Strawberry Daiquiris*

Strawberry Cream Dip*

Fresh Fruit Bowl

Strawberry Pie*

Coffee or Tea   Cognac

*See Strawberry Recipes
**See Peach Recipes

Strawberry Daiquiri

3 cups (1½ pt.) strawberries, hulled and coarsely
    chopped
6 ounces rum or orange juice
1 ounce lime juice
¼ cup (1¼ oz.) powdered sugar
chopped ice, as needed

Place strawberries, rum or orange juice, lime juice, and
powdered sugar in a blender container. Add chopped ice
until almost full. Blend slowly until mixture becomes
thick and ice is distributed evenly.

Strawberry Lemonade

4 cups (2 pt.) strawberries, hulled and coarsely
    chopped
1½ cups (9½ oz.) sugar
3 cups (24 fl. oz.) water
1½ cups (12 fl. oz.) lemon juice
crushed ice, as needed
whole strawberries, as needed

Place strawberries in a blender. Puree. In a saucepan,
combine sugar and water. Heat slowly until sugar dissolves. Mix with strawberry puree. Add lemon juice.
Chill. To serve, pour into chilled glasses. Add ice and
garnish with whole strawberries.

Strawberry Thickshakes

2 cups (1 pt.) strawberries, hulled and coarsely
    chopped
1 pint vanilla ice cream, softened
4 whole strawberries

Place strawberries in a blender. Puree. Add ice cream
and blend until smooth. Freeze for 1 hour in blender container. To serve, blend for a few more seconds, spoon into
tall glasses, and garnish with whole strawberries

Strawberry Bread

½ cup (4 fl. oz.) butter
1 cup (7 oz.) sugar
1 teaspoon vanilla
1 tablespoon lemon juice
3 eggs
2 cups (10 oz.) all-purpose flour
½ teaspoon salt
¾ teaspoon cream of tartar
½ teaspoon baking soda
½ cup (4 fl. oz.) sour cream
1 cup (8 oz.) pureed strawberries

Preheat oven to 350° F. (180° C.).
    Cream butter and sugar. Add vanilla and lemon juice
and beat until fluffy. Add eggs one at a time. Sift together
flour, salt, cream of tartar, and baking soda. Mix together
sour cream and strawberries. Alternately fold flour mixture and strawberry mixture into egg mixture.
    Pour into a 9 by 5 inch (23 by 13 cm.) loaf pan and bake
for 1 hour.

Ruby Game Hens

4 Cornish game hens
salt and pepper, to taste
4 cups (2 pt.) strawberries, hulled
3 tablespoons cornstarch
½ cup (4 fl. oz.) water
⅔ cup (5⅓ fl. oz.) orange juice
2 tablespoons lemon juice

Preheat oven to 350° F. (180° C.).
Wash game hens and season with salt and pepper.
Place in a roasting pan. Mash strawberries. Drain, reserving 1½ cups (12 fl. oz.) juice, and set pulp aside. In a bowl, combine cornstarch and water and mix until smooth. Add strawberry juice, orange juice, and lemon juice. Mix well and add strawberry pulp. Pour sauce over hens and roast, basting frequently with sauce, for 1½ hours, or until done.

Strawberry Fondue

1 cup (6 oz.) semi-sweet chocolate chips
3 tablespoons milk (optional)
1 tablespoon orange liqueur
2 cups (1 pt.) strawberries, with stems

Over low heat, melt chocolate. Add milk, if used, and orange liqueur. Holding stems, dip berries completely into chocolate mixture and place on waxed paper. Chill, and serve when cold.

Strawberry Cream Dip

⅓ cup (3 oz.) cream cheese
½ cup (2½ oz.) powdered sugar
1 tablespoon orange liqueur or milk
2 cups (1 pt.) strawberries, with stems

Mix cream cheese, powdered sugar, and enough liqueur or milk to make a good dip. Wash strawberries and allow guests to dip them in cheese mixture.

Strawberry Sorbet

1 cup (7 oz.) sugar
1 cup (8 fl. oz.) water
6 cups (3 pt.) strawberries, hulled and coarsely
    chopped
2 tablespoons lemon juice
2 tablespoons orange liqueur (optional)

Combine sugar and water in a small saucepan. Heat until sugar is dissolved. Chill. Puree strawberries and chill. Combine all ingredients and finish in an ice cream maker.

Strawberries Romanoff

4 cups (2 pt.) strawberries, hulled
⅓ cup (2⅔ fl. oz.) orange liqueur
1 cup (8 fl. oz.) heavy cream
⅓ cup (2¼ oz.) sugar

Combine strawberries and liqueur. Marinate for 30 minutes. Puree half the berries. Whip cream until soft peaks form; add sugar and beat until mixture mounds. Fold puree into cream mixture. Spoon puree over whole berries.

Berry Elegant Pie

½ tablespoon unflavored gelatin
¼ cup (2 fl. oz.) water
⅓ cup (3 oz.) cream cheese, softened
6 tablespoons powdered sugar
1 teaspoon vanilla
1 cup (8 fl. oz.) heavy cream
¾ cup (6 fl. oz.) plain yogurt
1 9-inch (23-cm.) pie shell, cooked and cooled
2 cups strawberries, hulled and halved
¼ cup (2 fl. oz.) strawberry jelly, melted

In a small saucepan, combine gelatin with water and dissolve over low heat; set aside. In a large mixing bowl, beat cream cheese with powdered sugar and vanilla until smooth; add cream. Beat until soft peaks form. Add dissolved gelatin and yogurt; beat until stiff. Pour into pie shell and chill 3 hours. Before serving, arrange berries on top. Drizzle jelly over berries.

Strawberry Pie

Glaze:

> 1 cup (6 oz.) strawberries, hulled and sliced
> ½ cup (3½ oz.) sugar
> dash salt
> ½ cup (4 fl. oz.) water
> 1½ teaspoons cornstarch
> 1 tablespoon lemon juice

Combine strawberries, sugar, salt, and ¼ cup (2 fl. oz.) of water in a saucepan. Bring to a boil and cook 3 minutes. Mix cornstarch with remaining water and stir until well combined. Slowly stir into strawberries and cook, stirring, until thick. Add lemon juice. Set aside.

Filling:

> ⅓ cup (3 oz.) cream cheese, softened
> 3 tablespoons milk
> 1 9-inch (23-cm.) pie shell, baked and cooled
> 2 cups strawberries, hulled

Beat cream cheese with milk until very smooth. Turn mixture into pie shell and cover with half of the glaze. Arrange strawberries, stem end down, on top. Spoon remaining glaze over strawberries. Chill for at least 2 hours.

SECTION
2

VEGETABLES

8 | ARTICHOKES
Let Them Eat Flowers

Let's get to know the chokes!

In case you haven't guessed, the "chokes" are artichokes; that's the term artichoke farmers almost invariably use when referring to their product. And remember, when you eat one of their chokes, you're not eating an ordinary vegetable, you're dining on a flower. The artichoke leaves (the things you pull through your teeth) are actually the petals of a flower, and the fleshy heart of the artichoke corresponds to the base of the flower's head.

But whatever it's called, you're eating a gourmet's delight at a cost of from 8 to 56 calories, depending on the size of the artichoke and the stage at which it was picked.

And the choke contributes a variety of useful vitamins and minerals.

Artichokes grow all year round, but the heaviest production is in April and May. That is certainly the time to buy them at the best price.

Lloyd Stolich, of the California Artichoke Advisory Board, has some tips on getting the most for your money. Look for artichokes with firm, solid heads and tightly closed leaves. If the leaves are starting to spread, the choke's not as fresh as it should be, and if it doesn't feel slightly heavy, it has lost some of its moisture and has started to wilt."

Pat Boutonnet, wife of an artichoke farmer, feels that consumers would do well to follow Stolich's advice carefully, because many produce managers are not yet familiar with the best way to store chokes. "I see big, gorgeous, prize chokes sitting out on display, and I can't stand it because I know they're not going to last as long as they could. They should be kept refrigerated and moist."

What's the best method for home storage? Pat Boutonnet says they should be rinsed off (to add some moisture), and then stored in the vegetable crisper or in a plastic bag sealed with a twistem and kept refrigerated. "They'll keep for a couple of weeks this way."

Cooking artichokes is simple. Pull off the lower outer leaves; then cut off the stem at the base. With kitchen scissors or a sharp knife, snip off the tips of the remaining leaves. Then stand each choke upright in a deep saucepan. Add two to three inches of boiling water and one-quarter teaspoon salt for each artichoke. A tablespoon of lemon juice will prevent darkening and a few drops of salad oil will make the leaves glisten. Cover the pot and boil gently, from thirty to forty-five minutes, or until the base can be pierced easily with a fork. When they are done, lift out the cooked artichokes and turn them upside down to drain. Finally, spread the leaves apart and remove the fuzz or thistle portion from the center, using a metal spoon.

Eating artichokes is fun—they're a great finger food. Just pull off the leaves one at a time and, holding onto the base, dip the fleshy end into a sauce. With your teeth, scrape off the edible "inside" of each leaf and discard the rest. When you get to the thistle—if it hasn't already been removed—scoop it out with a spoon and prepare to savor the best part of all, the tender heart.

Large artichokes make an impressive dish, but don't overlook the baby artichokes, advises artichoke specialist Dr. Vince Rubatsky. "The smaller ones are tenderer, and in Europe, people prefer them by such a wide margin that there's hardly a market for American-style large artichokes," says Rubatsky. Fortunately for us, more and more small artichokes will soon be marketed in this country.

To use the small artichokes, trim the tops of the leaves and then cut the artichokes in half lengthwise. Add them to stews for a wonderful flavor, or boil them and add to scrambled eggs or an omelette. Or marinate boiled baby artichokes in salad dressing and serve on toothpicks as appetizers.

Recipes sometimes call for artichoke pulp. To obtain the tender pulp, boil large artichokes until well done, then scrape the fleshy part from the base of the leaves and rub the bottom through a sieve. About four large artichokes will yield a cup (eight ounces) of pulp. To simplify the process, place cooked artichoke hearts in a blender and process on high for about half a minute.

In any event, do try artichokes. You'll be missing out on one of nature's most delicious flowers if you don't!

Artichokes in the Menu

SUPPER

Garlichokes*

Artichokes and Spaghetti*

Hot Crusty Italian Bread and Butter

Fresh Corn Salad**

Artichoke Pie*

Coffee or Tea

*See Artichoke Recipes
**See Corn Recipes

Artichoke Sunflower

This unique appetizer is as tasty as it is attractive.

1 large artichoke, cooked
⅓ cup (3 oz.) cream cheese
¼ teaspoon garlic powder
¼ teaspoon onion powder
¼ teaspoon hot pepper seasoning
2 tablespoons cream
¼ pound small shrimp, cooked
paprika, as needed

Remove all leaves from the artichoke. Set aside those that are firm enough to handle and that have an edible portion on the ends. Cut artichoke heart into quarters. Blend cream cheese with garlic and onion powders, hot pepper seasoning, and enough cream to make a smooth paste. Spread filling on the tip of each reserved leaf. Place one shrimp on top of filling and dust with paprika. Arrange prepared leaves in concentric circles on a round tray to resemble an open sunflower. Place quartered artichoke heart in the center.

Artichoke Loaf

16 to 18 small artichokes
1½ teaspoons butter
1 onion, chopped
salt and pepper, to taste
½ cup (4 fl oz.) water
3 slices bread, soaked in milk
3 eggs
½ cup (2 oz.) Parmesan cheese, grated

Preheat oven to 325° F. (165° C.).

Trim artichokes and slice finely. Melt butter in a saucepan; add onion and sauté for 5 minutes. Add artichokes, salt, and pepper, and stir. Add water and cover to steam for 8 minutes. Combine bread, eggs, and Parmesan cheese in a large bowl. Add steamed artichokes, stir well, and pour mixture into a buttered 6 by 8 inch (15 by 20 cm.) casserole. Bake for 45 minutes. To serve, cut into squares.

Artichokes with Ricotta-Mushroom Filling

8 large artichokes
1 tablespoon lemon juice
1½ cups (4 oz.) mushrooms, chopped
1 slice white bread, broken into small pieces
1 clove garlic, minced
½ tablespoon parsley, chopped
2 eggs
1 cup (8 oz.) ricotta cheese
salt and pepper, to taste
olive oil
Parmesan cheese, grated

Preheat oven to 350° F. (180° C.).

To prepare each artichoke for filling, remove the tough outer leaves, turn artichoke upside down and press down firmly, then cut off the top half. Trim the stem flush with the bottom, then with a small spoon scoop out the fibrous center leaves. Drop into a bowl of water to which 1 tablespoon lemon juice has been added.

Combine mushrooms, bread, garlic, parsley, eggs, ricotta, salt, and pepper. Fill artichokes with mixture, heaping on top. Arrange chokes in a baking pan greased with olive oil, sprinkle with Parmesan cheese, and bake for 30 minutes.

Artichoke Quiche

6 baby artichokes, or enough to make 2½ cups
1 teaspoon lemon juice
½ teaspoon salt
2 tablespoons butter
1 clove garlic, minced
1 medium onion, chopped
½ cup (4 fl oz.) half-and-half
½ cup (4 fl oz.) sour cream
¼ cup (1 oz.) fresh parsley, chopped
4 eggs
2 cups (16 oz.) Swiss cheese, shredded
1 teaspoon salt
⅛ teaspoon pepper
¼ cup (2 oz.) ham, finely chopped
2 9-inch (23-cm.) unbaked pie shells.

Preheat oven to 425° F. (220° C.).

Trim tops and stems from artichoke. Place chokes in saucepan with water to cover. Add lemon juice and salt and cook until tender. Drain, cool, and chop. You should have about 2½ cups chopped artichokes. Set aside.

In a saucepan, melt butter and sauté garlic and onion until soft. In a bowl, mix together half-and-half, sour cream, parsley, and eggs, and beat until well blended. Add onion mixture, cheese, artichokes, salt, pepper, and ham. Mix thoroughly. Pour into pie shells. Bake in 425° F. (220° C.) oven for 15 minutes. Reduce temperature to 350° F. (180° C.) and bake 35 minutes longer, or until set.

Garlichokes

6 medium artichokes
½ teaspoon salt
½ cup (4 fl oz.) olive oil
¼ cup (2 fl oz.) lemon juice
6 cloves garlic, minced
½ cup (2 oz.) parsley, chopped
½ teaspoon salt
dash pepper
2 cloves garlic, minced
1 egg yolk
1 tablespoon lemon juice
1 cup (8 fl oz.) mayonnaise

Wash and trim artichokes and set them snugly in a pan stem-end down. Pour boiling water over them to cover, add salt, cover and cook for 35 or 40 minutes, or until tender. Drain well. When cool, scoop out and discard center choke.

Combine oil, ¼ cup (2 fl oz.) lemon juice, 6 cloves garlic, parsley, salt, and pepper. Return artichokes to pan and pour oil and lemon mixture over, coating each artichoke. Simmer for 10 minutes. Allow to cool.

Place 2 cloves garlic, egg yolk, 1 tablespoon lemon juice, and ¼ cup (2 oz.) mayonnaise into blender. Whisk until smooth. Fold mixture into remaining mayonnaise.

To serve, fill artichoke centers with sauce. Garnish with sieved egg yolk or lemon wedges, if desired.

Chicken and Artichokes

6 large artichokes
1½ teaspoons salt
1 tablespoon lemon juice
½ pound bulk pork sausage
¼ cup (1½ oz.) onion, finely chopped
1 clove garlic, crushed
½ cup (4 oz.) rice
1¾ cups (14 fl oz.) chicken broth
⅛ teaspoon saffron
2 cups (16 oz.) chicken, cooked and cubed
½ cup (4 oz.) pimiento-stuffed olives, sliced
¾ cup (6 fl oz.) butter
¾ cup (6 fl oz.) dry sherry

Wash and trim artichokes and place in a saucepan. Add 2 to 3 inches boiling water, salt, and lemon juice. Cook for 30 to 40 minutes, until tender. Remove the fibrous center leaves. Keep chokes warm.

Meanwhile, in a large frying pan, cook sausage until brown. Remove, reserving 1 tablespoon drippings. Sauté onion and garlic in same pan until onion is crisp-tender. Add rice, broth, and saffron. Cover and cook over medium heat for 15 to 20 minutes, until tender. Add chicken, olives, and sausage. Heat until hot. Stuff artichokes with mixture.

For sauce, melt butter and sherry in a small saucepan. Simmer for 5 minutes.

To eat, remove leaves one at a time and dip into sauce.

Artichokes and Spaghetti

8 2-inch (5-cm.) to 3-inch (8-cm.) artichokes
1 teaspoon lemon juice
½ teaspoon salt
½ pound Italian sausage, crumbled
¼ cup (2 fl oz.) olive oil
2 tablespoons butter
2 cloves garlic, chopped
½ cup (3 oz.) onion, chopped
4 tomatoes, peeled and chopped
½ cup (4 fl oz.) white wine
¼ teaspoon dried basil
¼ teaspoon dried oregano
½ teaspoon sugar
salt and pepper, to taste
1 pound spaghetti, cooked
1 cup (4 oz.) Parmesan cheese, grated

Trim tops and stems from artichokes. Place chokes in saucepan with water to cover. Add lemon juice and salt and boil until just tender, approximately 30 minutes. Drain, cool, and halve, removing the fibrous center leaves. Set aside.

In a heavy pan, brown sausage. Remove and drain. In the same pan, heat oil and butter. Sauté garlic and onion until golden. Add tomatoes, wine, basil, oregano, and sugar. Simmer for 10 minutes. Add artichokes, salt, and pepper. Simmer for 15 minutes.

Serve on spaghetti with Parmesan cheese.

Artichoke Nut Chiffon Cake

2 cups (10 oz.) all-purpose flour
1½ cups (10½ oz.) sugar
1 teaspoon salt
1 tablespoon baking powder
½ cup (4 fl oz.) vegetable oil
7 eggs, separated
½ cup (4 oz.) artichoke pulp*
½ cup (2 oz.) almonds, finely chopped
½ cup (4 fl oz.) cold water
¼ cup (2 fl oz.) almond liqueur
1 teaspoon vanilla
½ teaspoon cream of tartar
¼ cup (1¼ oz.) powdered sugar

Preheat oven to 325° F. (165° C.).

Sift together flour, sugar, salt, and baking powder. Make a well in center. Add, in the following order, oil, egg yolks, artichoke pulp, almonds, water, liqueur, and vanilla. Beat for 1 minute, or until smooth. In a large bowl, beat egg whites and cream of tartar until stiff peaks form. Slowly pour egg yolk mixture over egg whites and gently fold together. Do not stir. Pour into a 10-inch (25-cm.) tube pan and bake for 65 to 70 minutes, or until top springs back when lightly touched. Immediately invert pan and allow cake to cool. Loosen cake from sides with a spatula.

To serve, dust top with powdered sugar or frost with a whipped cream fosting.

*To prepare pulp, see text on artichokes, p. 76

Artichoke Pie

2 cups (16 oz.) artichoke pulp*
½ cup (3½ oz.) sugar
3 eggs
1 cup (8 fl oz.) milk
1 teaspoon salt
1 teaspoon cinnamon
½ teaspoon nutmeg
¼ teaspoon cloves
¼ teaspoon allspice
1 9-inch (23-cm.) pie shell, unbaked
1 cup (8 fl oz.) heavy cream

Preheat oven to 450° F. (230° C.).

In a bowl, combine artichoke pulp, sugar, eggs, milk, salt, cinnamon, nutmeg, cloves, and allspice. Mix well and pour into pie shell. Bake in a 450° F. (230° C.) oven for 10 minutes. Reduce temperature to 375° F. (190° C.) and bake 20 minutes longer, or until firm.

To serve, whip cream and use to garnish.

*To prepare pulp, see text on artichokes, p. 76

9 | ASPARAGUS
Great Green Grass

"That's a pretty good crop of grass!"

The speaker is a cool, with-it-looking guy, and as you sneak a quick sideways glance at him, you know this man isn't talking about his lawn.

But if the speaker's name is Bill De Paoli, you can be pretty sure the grass he's talking about isn't marijuana either. To an asparagus man, "grass" means asparagus.

De Paoli isn't exaggerating when he says the crop he's pointing at is a good one. In fact, for the whole asparagus industry, the best is just to come.

The reason is a revolution in the asparagus industry. Very recently, the first commercially available hybrid asparagus seed has been introduced and the new hybrid is almost twice as productive as preceding varieties. On top of this, the hybrid is blessed with an excellent flavor.

Asparagus takes a while to get started—three years from seed to commercial production. Once a plant is of producing age, it can form ten to twelve spears each year over a period of almost a decade. Harvesting those spears is a tricky business, though, for they must be picked at just the right size to assure maximum flavor and tenderness. The grower aims to catch the asparagus when the spear is about nine inches long; but if the day is warm and the soil damp, asparagus can grow seven and one-half inches in a single day. (It's a fact that asparagus is the fastest growing commercial vegetable.) Since all asparagus harvesting is done by hand, catching the plant at just the right moment can mean inspecting a plant twice a day. Imagine what the typical asparagus grower is up against, on a warm day, when he has two and one-half million plants to look out for.

Once the nine-inch shoots are picked, they are packed upright on damp paper in a box ten and one-half inches high. The extra one and a half inches is to allow the plant growing room. Since the plant is still alive, it will keep growing, and if stored for a while, it will elongate and fill the headroom in the box. Growers keep cut asparagus chilled to prevent this, because the less the plant elongates, the less fiber it will produce.

If you ever want proof that an asparagus spear continues to grow after cutting, leave one in your refrigerator for four to five days. Then, notice how the tip is bending upwards. Asparagus spears tend to grow away from the center of gravity, and that bending is the plant's actual growth away from the earth.

At the supermarket, buy asparagus with tightly closed tips and straight, rounded stalks. If the spears are wilted or flat, pass them by. They've lost valuable moisture and will be tough.

For home storage, De Paoli advises refrigerating the spears along with a damp paper towel, in a plastic bag sealed with a twistem. "The sooner they're eaten, the better their flavor and the more tender they are," advises De Paoli.

Before cooking, snap off the tough end by grasping the stalk with both hands and bending. The stalk will break at just the point where the tough portion meets the tender portion. "But don't throw away the tough portion!" insists De Paoli. "Peel off the skin with a potato peeler and use what's left in soups or casseroles."

De Paoli doesn't want us to waste any of the nutrients in our asparagus. And he has a point. Asparagus is outstanding as a source for vitamins A and C, and it also contains rutin, a substance critical for circulatory health. And there are just *3 calories* in a half-inch cooked spear!

❀

*Asparagus
in the Menu*

LUNCH

California Chardonnay

Pick-Up Peach Salads**

Asparagus Soup*

Sourdough Rolls and Butter

Deep-Fried Asparagus*

Peach Cake**

Coffee or Tea

*See Asparagus Recipes
**See Peach Recipes

❀

Deep-Fried Asparagus

1 pound asparagus
⅔ cup (3¼ oz.) all-purpose flour
½ teaspoon salt
⅔ cup (5⅓ fl. oz.) milk
1 egg, separated
¼ teaspoon cream of tartar
vegetable oil, as needed
garlic salt, to taste

Break off white ends of asparagus and set aside for another use. Cut remaining portions of spears into 1½-inch (4-cm.) pieces.

Combine flour, salt, milk, and egg yolk. Mix well. Beat egg white until peaks form, add cream of tartar, and continue to beat until very stiff. Fold into flour mixture.

To cook, pour oil to depth of 2½ inches (6½ cm.) into a wok. Heat to 375° F. (187° C.). Dip asparagus pieces into batter and fry in oil until light brown. Sprinkle lightly with garlic salt while frying. When asparagus pieces are done, remove, and drain on paper towels.

Rice and Asparagus Casserole

1 tablespoon butter
1 tablespoon vegetable oil
1 onion, chopped
1 pound asparagus, cut into 1-inch (2½-cm.) pieces, white ends discarded
1 cup (8 oz.) rice
2 cups (16 fl. oz.) chicken or beef stock
1 cup (4 oz.) Parmesan cheese, grated

Melt butter and oil in a saucepan. Sauté onion and asparagus for 5 to 10 minutes. Add rice and sauté until light brown. Add stock, cover, and cook for 20 to 25 minutes, until rice is tender. Stir cheese into hot rice and mix gently until ingredients are combined.

Asparagus Soup

1½ pounds asparagus
1 tablespoon olive oil
1 tablespoon butter
2 cloves garlic, chopped
1 onion, chopped
4 cups (32 fl. oz.) beef or chicken stock
2 tablespoons cornstarch
2 cups (16 fl. oz.) half-and-half
salt and pepper, to taste

Break off white ends of asparagus, and put aside for another use. Chop spears into 2-inch (5-cm.) pieces. Bring a large pan of water to a boil. Add asparagus and boil until tender, approximately 15 minutes. Remove from water, reserving water and a few tips. Puree stalks in a small amount of water and set aside.

Heat oil and butter in a large pan. Add garlic and onion and sauté until limp. Add stock. In a cup, combine cornstarch and a small amount of asparagus water. Slowly add to stock and cook until slightly thickened. Add pureed asparagus, half-and-half, and remaining asparagus water, if desired. Season with salt and pepper, and add reserved asparagus tips. Heat until warmed, but do not allow to boil.

Asparagus Sauté

This special recipe uses the white ends of asparagus stalks, so often discarded by the cook, to produce a unique and tasty vegetable dish.

1 to 2 pounds asparagus
2 tablespoons olive oil
1 onion, sliced
2½ cups (½ lb.) mushrooms, sliced
salt and pepper, to taste

Snap off the bottom 3 or 4 inches (8 to 10 cm.) of each asparagus stalk. Save the tip and center for another recipe. With a sharp knife, peel the white ends of the asparagus and slice lengthwise. Heat oil in a frying pan. When oil is hot, add asparagus and onion. Cook until almost tender, approximately 20 minutes. Add mushrooms and continue to cook until just done. Season with salt and pepper.

Pickled Asparagus

8 cups (64 fl. oz.) water
5 cups (40 fl. oz.) white vinegar
7 tablespoons salt
2 teaspoons pickling spice, without cloves
2 to 3 pounds asparagus, with white ends removed
garlic cloves, as needed

Combine water, vinegar, salt, and pickling spice. Boil, uncovered, for 15 minutes. Strain, and keep hot.

Bring a large pan of water to a boil. Cook asparagus for 2 to 2½ minutes; remove and immediately plunge them into ice water to cool. Drain and pat dry.

Pack asparagus in jars, arranging as desired. Add 4 cloves garlic to each jar, pour in hot brine, and seal as manufacturer directs. Allow to ripen for at least 2 weeks before serving.

Asparagus Frittata

1 large onion, chopped
2 tablespoons butter
1 pound asparagus, cut into 1-inch pieces, white ends discarded
6 eggs, beaten
2 tablespoons parsley, chopped
2 tablespoons Parmesan cheese, grated
salt and pepper, to taste

Preheat oven to 350° F. (180° C.).

In a 10-inch (25-cm.) oven-proof frying pan, sauté onion in butter until translucent. Add asparagus and stir fry for 1 minute. In a bowl, mix eggs, parsley, Parmesan cheese, salt, and pepper. Pour egg mixture over asparagus mixture. Bake for about 20 minutes, or until set.

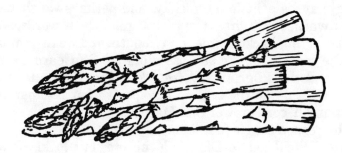

10 | CORN
Its Roots Go Back a Long Way

This may be a little bit sneaky, and perhaps we should
have warned you first, but as you read these words, we
are traveling back in time to Plymouth, and we're aiming
for the year 1620. The purpose of our trip? To learn about
corn and the Pilgrim Fathers. We're lucky, because we
have with us on the trip an unexpected but fascinating
companion, corn grower Dan Macedo.

The reason Dan is so fascinating is that . . .

Wait! We'll get to Dan in a minute, but look! We've
arrived! We've undershot a bit, it's 1623, but we've come
at the time of year "when the oak tree leaves are as big as

mice ears." That's an Indian expression meaning it's time to plant corn.

As we walk down the dirt paths between the few houses, we notice an extraordinary sight: every dog in the settlement is hobbling around with one forepaw fastened to its neck.

"Why would anyone do such a thing," you demand, partly horrified, but also more than a little curious.

The answer is, to protect the corn. The colonists have learned to copy the Indian method of fertilizing their corn by burying a small fish among the four kernels that go into each little hill. But, unfortunately, the colony's dogs have a taste for fish, and tying one forepaw is the only way to keep them from digging up the fish.

Dan Macedo is intrigued. Although he's a corn farmer, he's studied marine biology, and the notion of planting the corn with decaying fish catches his attention.

"You know," he comments, "probably the biggest factor that corn removes from the soil is nitrogen. Fish, on the other hand, are extremely high in nitrogen. Interesting," he observes, "that the colonists and the Indians before them hit on just the right combination."

(For our benefit, Macedo points out that twentieth-century farmers solve the problem of nitrogen depletion by rotating their corn with alfalfa, which fixes nitrogen from the air and puts it back in the soil for the next crop of corn. They also supplement with additional nitrogen in the form of ammonium.)

The dogs, with their tied-up forepaws, aren't the only things to catch our attention. There's something else that has to do with corn, and we discover it as our party enters one of the primitive log houses. A woman in the far corner of the dirt-floored cabin is stirring a hot cauldron. Peering into the steaming, whitish liquid, we can just make out a few kernels of corn, roiling around in the simmering brew. She explains that there are also ground hickory nuts and chestnuts cooking in there.

She's cooking up the Pilgrim's substitute for milk. Until next year, 1624, there will not be a single dairy animal in all of Plymouth, and hunger being the mother of invention, the Pilgrims have devised this broth as a substitute for milk for their children.

Although the Pilgrims can't know it, this corn and nut "milk" is an excellent protein source. Corn is low in two factors needed for complete protein (tryptophan and lysine) while nuts happen to have these factors in abundance. By putting the corn and nuts together, the Pilgrim mothers are providing their children with good, complete protein just as surely as if they were serving them cow's milk.

Leaving Plymouth, let's think just a bit further—back to 5000 B.C., in fact. We have something significant in common with Indians who lived in the Tehuacan Valley of Mexico about that time. Both we and they are—or were—corn eaters. The Tehuacan Indians seem to have been the very first to have brought corn under cultivation, and we Americans, since we eat twenty-eight pounds of it each year, have reason to be grateful to them.

But leaving history behind, let's return to the present. Today corn continues to be an important source of food energy, fiber, and, provided it's yellow corn, vitamin A. It also contains appreciable amounts of potassium, thiamine, niacin, and vitamin C. A medium-size ear has about 45 calories.

One thing to watch for when buying fresh corn is whether the corn is displayed in a single layer or whether it is piled high. As corn "breathes"—and it does, since it's living tissue after all—it gives off heat. The more heat surrounds it, the faster the chemical process of converting sugar to starch. A pile of corn can generate enough heat to affect the flavor.

If you are buying fresh corn, how do you pick a good ear? Look first at the stem end for a clue as to how long ago it was picked. Does it look fresh? Or dry and straw-like? Pull a small portion of the husk back to see if the kernels look tender and milky. Richard Stuhaan, a corn grower, says if it's corn you've grown yourself, you can tell when it's ready by piercing a kernel with your fingernail. "If it's watery, it's not ready. If it's milky, it's good. If it's like cream, it's perfect. But if it's gotten doughy, it's past its peak flavor."

And what about cooking it? Farmer's wife Linda Macedo says, "Keep your corn refrigerated until you're ready to cook it. Husk it, drop it in boiling water, and then cook for no more than one minute. It's done as soon as the 'milk' inside the kernels sets. Any cooking beyond that is only going to boil away the flavor." Linda seasons with nothing but salt, pepper, and butter.

We asked Linda if one minute wasn't an awfully short time to cook corn. Some old recipes, for instance, have directed that it be boiled for twenty minutes. Linda is horrified by the thought. "Heavens no," she insists, "some farmers like the true taste of corn so much they refuse to spoil it by cooking it at all!"

Corn
in the Menu

SUMMER LUNCH

California Sauvignon Blanc

Fresh Corn Appetizer Dip*

Tortilla Chips

Corn Omelet*

Whole Wheat Rolls and Butter

Fresh Tomato Summer Salad**

Cheese Wedges

Fresh Fruit

Iced Coffee or Tea

*See Corn Recipes
**See Tomato Recipes

Fresh Corn Appetizer Dip

⅓ cup (3 oz.) cream cheese, softened
1 tablespoon lemon juice
3 tablespoons heavy cream or sour cream
1 small clove garlic, mashed
1 teaspoon oregano leaves, crumbled
2 tablespoons pimiento, chopped
2 tablespoons green onion, chopped
1½ cups (9 oz.) corn kernels, cooked
½ teaspoon salt

In a small bowl, blend together cream cheese, lemon juice, heavy cream or sour cream, garlic, oregano, pimiento, and green onion. Add corn and salt. Stir to blend. Cover and refrigerate for at least 2 hours.

Kentucky Fried Corn

8 pieces bacon, cut into 1-inch (2½-cm.) squares
2 cups (12 oz.) corn kernels
2 cucumbers, thinly sliced
1 onion, minced
pinch sugar
1 egg, beaten
salt and pepper, to taste
2 tablespoons pimiento

Fry bacon and pour off all but 3 tablespoons of fat. Remove 3 tablespoons bacon and drain. Reserve. To pan, add corn, cucumbers, onion, sugar, egg, salt, and pepper. Sauté slowly for 30 minutes.

To serve, garnish with reserved bacon, crumbled, and pimiento.

Fresh Corn Salad

3 cups (18 oz.) corn kernels, cooked
1½ cups (9 oz.) celery, sliced thinly
1 red or green bell pepper, chopped
3 green onions, sliced
2 tablespoon sweet pickle, chopped
⅓ cup (2⅔ fl. oz.) mayonnaise
¼ cup (2 fl. oz.) sour cream
1 tablespoon vinegar
½ teaspoon salt, or more to taste
½ teaspoon Worcestershire sauce
⅛ teaspoon pepper
½ teaspoon Dijon mustard
¼ teaspoon basil leaves, crumbled
lettuce leaves, as needed

In a bowl, combine corn, celery, half the bell pepper, onions, and pickle. Cover and chill. In a small bowl, combine mayonnaise, sour cream, vinegar, salt, Worcestershire sauce, pepper, mustard, and basil; cover and chill.

Before serving, combine vegetables with dressing. Serve on lettuce leaves garnished with remaining bell pepper.

Fresh Corn Soufflé

¼ cup (2 fl. oz.) butter
¼ cup (1¼ oz.) all-purpose flour
⅔ cup (5⅓ fl. oz.) milk
2 cups (12 oz.) corn kernels, cooked and sieved
3 eggs, separated
½ teaspoon salt
½ cup (3 oz.) grated Cheddar cheese
2 tablespoons green pepper, chopped

Preheat oven to 350° F. (180° C.).

Melt butter. Add flour and mix to a smooth paste. Cook for 1 minute, stirring constantly. Add milk and corn and cook until thick. Remove from heat. Beat egg yolks. Add to corn mixture, along with salt, cheese, and green pepper. Beat egg whites until stiff and fold into corn mixture. Pour into greased baking dish and bake for 30 minutes. Serve immediately.

Cheesy Corn Bake

3 tablespoons butter
2 tablespoons all-purpose flour
½ teaspoon salt
¼ teaspoon pepper
1 teaspoon taco sauce
½ cup (4 fl. oz.) milk
½ cup (4 fl. oz.) sour cream
2 cups (12 oz.) corn kernels, uncooked
½ cup (3 oz.) Monterey Jack or other mild cheese, shredded
½ cup (3 oz.) Cheddar cheese, shredded
½ cup (2 oz.) bread crumbs, buttered

Preheat oven to 350° F. (180° C.).

Melt butter. Stir in flour, salt, pepper, and taco sauce. Cook over low heat, stirring constantly, until smooth and bubbly. Remove from heat. Stir in milk and sour cream. Cook over low heat until sauce thickens. Do not allow to boil.

Stir in corn and cheeses. Spoon batter into buttered 1-quart casserole. Sprinkle with crumbs. Bake for 30 minutes.

Scalloped Fresh Corn

3 cups (18 oz.) corn kernels, uncooked
½ cup (3 oz.) ripe olives, sliced
½ to ¾ cup (3 oz. to 4 oz.) Monterey Jack or mild
    Cheddar cheese, diced
¾ teaspoon salt
¼ teaspoon pepper
1½ tablespoons butter

Preheat oven to 350° F. (180° C.).

Combine corn with olives, cheese, salt, and pepper. Pour into a shallow 1½-quart (48-oz.) to 2-quart (64-oz.) casserole. Dot with butter. Bake uncovered for 25 minutes, or until cheese is melted.

Corn Omelet

6 eggs, separated
2 cups (12 oz.) corn kernels, cooked
1 teaspoon salt
dash pepper
2 tablespoons parsley, chopped
½ teaspoon ground cumin
4 tablespoons butter, melted

Preheat oven to 350° F. (180° C.).

Combine egg yolks with corn, salt, pepper, parsley, cumin, and 2 tablespoons of the butter. Heat remaining butter in an oven-proof frying pan. Beat egg whites until stiff. Fold corn mixture into egg whites and spoon mixture into frying pan. Cook over low heat until mixture is set around edge of pan and golden on the bottom. Place in oven and bake 15 to 20 minutes, or until just set.

Mexican Corn on the Cob

½ cup (4 fl. oz.) butter, melted
2 tablespoons chili powder
2 teaspoons paprika
salt and pepper, to taste
4 to 6 ears corn, husked

Preheat oven to 350° F. (180° C.) or prepare barbecue.

Mix together butter, chili powder, paprika, salt, and pepper. Spread on corn, wrap in heavy foil, and seal well. Place in a baking dish and bake or barbecue for 1 hour, or until corn is tender.

Corn and Tomato Chowder

2 cups (12 oz.) corn kernels, uncooked
1 cup (8 oz.) tomatoes, diced
1 cup (6 oz.) celery, diced
2½ cups (20 fl. oz.) water
1 teaspoon salt
2 tablespoons butter
3 tablespoons all-purpose flour
2 cups (16 fl. oz.) milk
½ cup (3 oz.) Cheddar cheese, shredded
1 green pepper, finely chopped
salt and pepper, to taste

Combine corn, tomatoes, celery, water, and salt. Bring to boil and simmer 30 minutes. Meanwhile, in another pan, melt butter and blend in flour. Cook for 1 minute. Add milk and cook, stirring, until thickened. Add sauce to cooked vegetable mixture. Stir in cheese, green pepper, salt, and pepper, and heat until warmed through.

11 | DRIED BEANS
A Big Bargain

Beans may be nutritious, inexpensive, and tasty, but they are, er ... well, windy. If beans have this effect on you, take heart, for the United States Department of Agriculture has come to your rescue. Recently completed research has isolated important factors in beans that cause "windiness," and we now know what to do to avoid it.

The problem is, beans contain certain carbohydrates called oligosaccharides, which the stomach is unable to digest. But if beans are soaked for twenty-four hours, 90 percent of these villainous oligosaccharides are leached out and dissolved in the soak water. When you throw away the soak water, you're also getting rid of most of the problem.

For a quicker way to accomplish the same thing, add three cups of hot water to each cup of dry beans, heat, and boil for three minutes, and then cover and set aside for an hour. Drain, rinse, and the beans are ready to cook.

Incidentally, you don't have to worry about wasting vitamins in the soaking and rinsing water. By coincidence, the ones you pour out happen to be the very ones that would be destroyed by cooking later on anyway.

While you can skip the soaking if you're short on time, the USDA study showed that this step not only helps prevent gas, it also improves the beans' flavor, texture, digestibility, and appearance. Finally, it saves energy, for soaked beans require much less cooking time.

Nutritionally and economically, beans are a bargain. The USDA lists the foods that provide the most protein per dollar and—to the bean farmer's everlasting delight— beans top the list. Depending on the variety, beans contain from 21 to 27 percent protein.

And that's not the end of the protein story. Of the eight essential amino acids needed to make a complete protein, beans have seven. They lack only methionine. Grains are rich in this factor, so if you eat your beans with a corn taco, rice, or a slice of bread, you are getting the protein you need just as surely as if you are eating a steak. When our New England forebears served corn bread and baked beans for supper every Saturday, they were doing precisely the right thing nutritionally, although they couldn't have known why.

If the protein argument isn't enough to convince you that beans are a bargain, consider this. Dry beans are among the richest natural sources of the B-complex vitamins. For example, cooked blackeye beans are comparable to cooked liver or raw wheat germ with respect to folic acid. And a six-ounce serving of cooked large limas, black-eyes, or pink beans is better than brewer's yeast or wheat germ as a source of pyridoxine.

These B-complex vitamins perform an important function in the process that turns our food into energy and keeps digestive and nervous systems healthy. Beans are also high in calcium, iron, and potassium, which are important for strong bones and teeth, for building red blood cells, and for regulating the fluid balance of the body.

It's a curious fact, but beans are not only good for the people who eat them, they're also good for the soil that grows them. Says bean farmer Jack Osborne, "Beans trap nitrogen from the air and leave it in the soil for the next crop." Farmers don't have to use as much commercial fertilizer when they've grown beans.

Beans are truly a magic food. Once cooked, they can be kept in the refrigerator and then quickly served in dozens of different ways. Bean farmer Jim Andreas gives this advice for preparing your beans: "Inspect a one-pound bag of beans for damaged beans or foreign material. Put in a pot large enough for beans to expand two and one-half times, add six cups of cold water, and let stand overnight, or at least six hours. Do not refrigerate. Drain and discard water, then rinse once more. The beans are now ready to cook. Add six cups of hot water, two teaspoons of onion salt, one-fourth teaspoon garlic salt, and three bouillon cubes. Boil gently with lid tilted until desired tenderness is reached. This will be more or less an hour, depending on the variety of beans. They're ready to eat now, to be added to casseroles or salads."

Uncooked dried beans can be easily stored on the shelf. Once a package has been opened, just transfer the unused portion to an airtight glass or metal container. Cooked beans can be stored in the refrigerator for a day or two, or frozen for later use.

For an aid in keeping your nutritional values up and your food expenditures down, consider beans!

Beans
in the Menu

SUMMER LUNCH

California Rosé

Chilled Borscht with Beans*

Chilled Meat Loaf Slices*

French Rolls and Butter

Gherkins

Almond Slaw**

Almond Tea Cookies** and Sherbet

Coffee or Tea

*See Bean Recipes
**See Almond Recipes

Chili Bean Soup

2 cups (1 lb.) pink, red, or pinto beans
6 to 8 cups (48 to 64 fl. oz.) water, boiling
1 teaspoon garlic salt
1 teaspoon onion salt
¼ teaspoon thyme
¼ teaspoon marjoram
1 cup (8 fl. oz.) beef or chicken stock
3 tomatoes, peeled and seeded
1 cup (7 fl. oz.) green chili salsa
1 cup (8 fl. oz.) water, hot

Rinse and soak beans. Drain and empty them into a large pot. Add boiling water, garlic salt, onion salt, thyme, and marjoram. Cover and simmer for 2⅓ to 3 hours, or until beans are tender. During cooking add hot water, if needed, to keep beans moist. Remove 3 cups (24 oz.) beans and save for another use. Mash remaining beans in their liquid. Add stock, tomatoes, salsa, and hot water. Heat thoroughly, or until tomatoes are well cooked.

Borscht with Beans

8 cups (64 fl. oz.) beef stock
2 cups (12 oz.) raw beets, pared and coarsely grated
1 onion, chopped
2 cups (12 oz.) cabbage, coarsely shredded
1½ cups (4 oz.) pink beans, cooked and drained*
1 tablespoon butter
1 tablespoon lemon juice
salt and pepper, to taste
1 cup (8 fl. oz.) sour cream

In a large pot, bring stock to a boil. Add beets and onions and cook for 15 to 20 minutes, until tender. Add cabbage and beans. Cook for 10 minutes. Add butter, lemon juice, salt, and pepper.

To serve, garnish with sour cream.

*For cooking directions, see text on beans, p. 106.

Salinas Bean Bake

2 cups (1 lb.) pink beans
1 quart (32 fl. oz.) water
¼ cup (1½ oz.) onion, chopped
1 tablespoon butter
1 small ham hock
1 clove garlic, pressed
1 teaspoon celery salt
1 tablespoon cumin
¼ teaspoon ginger
1 teaspoon dry mustard
¼ cup (2 fl. oz.) butter
salt and pepper, to taste

Soak beans overnight. Drain. Bring water to boil in a large oven-proof casserole. Add beans and simmer for ½ hour.

Preheat oven to 300° F. (150° C.).

In a saucepan, sauté onion with 1 tablespoon butter. Add onion to the bean mixture along with the ham hock, garlic, celery salt, cumin, ginger, mustard, butter, salt, and pepper. Place casserole in oven and bake until beans are tender. Add water when needed as fluid is reduced by oven cooking. Alternatively, cook in a crock pot on high for 5 hours.

Mixed Bean Salad

Salad:

  3 cups (8 oz.) garbanzo beans, cooked and drained*
  3 cups (8 oz.) pink or kidney beans, cooked and
    drained*
  2 cups (5 oz.) small white beans, cooked and
    drained*

Mix together garbanzo beans, pink or kidney beans, and small white beans. Set aside.

Dressing:

  ⅔ cup (4½ oz.) sugar
  2 tablespoons cornstarch
  1 teaspoon onion salt
  ¼ teaspoon pepper
  ⅛ teaspoon garlic powder
  ½ cup (4 fl. oz.) cold water
  1½ cups (12 fl. oz.) boiling water
  ⅔ cup (5⅓ fl. oz.) vinegar from sweet pickles
  salt and pepper, to taste

In a saucepan, mix sugar, cornstarch, onion salt, pepper, and garlic powder. Add cold water and stir until smooth. Gradually stir in boiling water. Bring mixture to a boil, stirring until thick and clear. Blend in vinegar. Add dressing to beans, mixing gently. Add salt and pepper. Cover and chill overnight.

Garnish:

  lettuce, as needed
  tomato slices, as needed
  onion rings, as needed

To serve, drain off excess dressing, empty beans into a deep platter and garnish with lettuce, tomato slices, and onion rings.

*For cooking directions, see text on beans, p. 106.

Hearty Pink Beans

2 cups (1 lb.) pink beans
½ teaspoon onion powder
6 or 7 slices bacon, diced
1 onion, chopped
2 stalks celery, chopped
1 clove garlic, minced
½ cup (4 fl. oz.) tomato paste
1½ teaspoons chili powder
2 tablespoons sugar
1 tablespoon dry mustard
1 tablespoon vinegar
½ teaspoon salt, or more to taste
1 teaspoon pepper
10 cups (80 fl. oz.) cold water
1 pound ground beef or ground ham
¼ cup (2 fl. oz.) bourbon

Soak beans overnight in water. Drain. In a large heavy pot combine beans with onion powder, bacon, onion, celery, garlic, tomato paste, chili powder, sugar, mustard, vinegar, salt, pepper, and water. Simmer for several hours, until tender. An hour before serving, brown ground meat in a frying pan and add to bean mixture. Add bourbon, and allow to simmer until ready to serve.

Meat Loaf

1¼ pounds ground beef
¼ pound ground pork
¾ cup (2 oz.) beans, cooked and drained*
¼ cup (1½ oz.) onion, chopped
1 cup (4 oz.) bread crumbs
1½ teaspoons salt
¼ teaspoon pepper
2 eggs, beaten slightly
½ cup (4 fl. oz.) milk
2 tablespoons catsup
2 tablespoons butter
2 or 3 strips bacon, cut in squares

Preheat oven to 375° F. (190° C.).

Combine beef, pork, beans, onion, bread crumbs, salt, and pepper in a large bowl. Add eggs, milk, and catsup. Melt butter in a 9 by 5 inch (23 by 13 cm.) loaf pan, add to mixture, and mix well with fork. Pack into pan and top with bacon. Bake for 1 hour.

To serve, drain off liquid and slice. Excellent hot or cold.

*For cooking directions, see text on beans, p. 106.

Black-Eyed Chicken

This delightful and unusual dish can be made from start to finish in one skillet

    1 fryer chicken, disjointed
    seasoned all-purpose flour, as needed
    2 to 3 tablespoons vegetable oil
    2 to 3 tablespoons butter
    3 to 4 tablespoons onion, finely chopped
    ½ pound mushrooms, quartered
    ¼ teaspoon mixed fine herbs
    ½ cup (4 fl. oz.) dry white wine or chicken stock
    3 cups (8 oz.) black-eyed beans, cooked and
       drained*
    1 tomato, coarsely diced
    water or stock, as needed

Dry chicken pieces with paper towels, and coat with seasoned flour. Heat oil and butter in a large skillet and brown chicken slowly on both sides until golden brown. Remove from pan and keep warm.

To the skillet add more oil and butter, if needed, onions and mushrooms. Sauté for 10 minutes. Add fine herbs, wine or chicken stock, and beans. Bring to a boil. Arrange browned chicken over top, partially sinking pieces into beans. Scatter tomato over beans, add enough stock or water to just cover beans. Cover and simmer for 10 to 20 minutes, or until chicken is fork-tender.

*For cooking directions, see text on beans, p. 106.

Bockwurst and Bean Casserole

2 cups (1 lb.) small white beans
3 tablespoons butter
1 small onion, chopped
1 clove garlic, pressed
¼ cup (1½ oz.) green pepper, chopped
¼ cup (1½ oz.) celery, chopped
1 teaspoon dry mustard
½ teaspoon ginger
1 small ham hock
¼ cup (2 fl. oz.) butter
1 Bockwurst

Soak beans in water overnight. Drain. Place beans in large oven-proof casserole with enough water to cover. Bake in oven for 2 hours, or until beans are almost tender. Remove from oven.

Preheat oven to 300° F. (150° C.).

Melt 3 tablespoons butter in a saucepan. Sauté onions, garlic, pepper, and celery until transluscent. Add to bean mixture, along with mustard, ginger, ham hock, and ¼ cup butter. Return to oven and cook until tender.

Slice Bockwurst in ¼-inch (¾-cm.) slices, add to bean mixture, and continue baking until Bockwurst is tender. Add water occasionally, as needed.

12 | PUMPKINS
The S–p–o–o–k–y Squash

"Can I do it, can I, please?"

You look down at the little pleading face, and then you glance at the sharp carving knife you're holding, and you shake your head "no." The child is still much too young to carve a Jack O'Lantern, but maybe you can ease the disappointment a little by telling him or her the story behind the Hallowe'en pumpkin you're carving.

"Hundreds of years ago," you begin, "every Hallowe'en the people in Ireland used to carve s-p-o-o-k-y faces on turnips and potatoes."

"Why?" a little voice interrupts.

"They did it because they were remembering the story of a man who was supposed to be so stingy he was never even considered for Heaven, but he was also so mischievous that the Devil didn't want him in Hell either. The man, says the legend, was condemned to wander the earth with a lighted lantern until Judgment Day."

"But how did potatoes and turnips get to be Jack O'Lanterns?" your little listener is going to ask.

Here's your answer: "There was a potato famine in Ireland in the 1840s, and many Irish people came to this country so they'd have food to eat. They brought with them their Hallowe'en custom of carving scary faces, but here they found that pumpkins worked better than the other vegetables, especially when they could put a lighted candle inside the pumpkin."

There's a lot more you can tell your little ones about pumpkins. For instance, pumpkins had a lot to do with keeping the Pilgrims alive. Since pumpkins are easy to grow and store well—up to a year if kept cool and dry—the Pilgrims depended on them during lean periods.

They often served pumpkins roasted in slices with maple sugar, or baked after being cut in half and slathered with fresh-churned butter. For variety, they boiled them, made them into soup, or kneaded them with maize to make pancakes. There was also pumpkin pudding, pumpkin tarts, and even pumpkin beer, made by fermenting pumpkins with persimmons and maple sugar.

Neither the Pilgrims nor the Irish in the last century would have recognized the big carving pumpkins we have today. The seventy- to one-hundred-pound Big Max or Jack O'Lantern kinds are a recent development, and they are not particularly good for food.

"You could eat the big ones," says Gail Dick, a pumpkin grower, "but," she warns, "the flesh tends to be thick, watery, and tasteless." It's also not as nutritious because the pale insides of the carving pumpkin never develop as much vitamin A as the carrot-colored eating pumpkins.

The eating pumpkins—you can tell them by their relatively small size, around ten pounds or less—are a nutritious food source. A cup of mashed pumpkin contains 3400

International Units of vitamin A, or nearly 70 percent of an adult's Recommended Daily Allowance. A 3.5-ounce serving has 80 calories, 20 grams of carbohydrate, and 3 grams of protein.

According to the growers, how does one choose a good pumpkin on the vine? Gail Dick says, "First of all, you don't have to worry about getting a pumpkin at peak ripeness, the way you might with a pear or a tomato. A pumpkin can stay very good for months if kept cool and dry. Timing isn't critical, but do make sure you've got one that has no shriveling or traces of mold on it. It should feel heavy for its size, not light or spongy, which could indicate decay inside."

At home, pumpkins will store whole on the shelf for about a month. In the refrigerator they'll keep for up to four months. Fresh-cooked pumpkin stores in the refrigerator for four or five days.

Pumpkins are easy to prepare for cooking. Boil chopped and peeled pumpkin chunks in salted water until tender, for fifteen or twenty minutes, and then mash. Or bake pumpkin halves or chunks in a shallow pan at 350 degrees Fahrenheit (180 degrees Celsius) for an hour or so; then mash. A pound of pumpkin, cooked and mashed, will yield approximately a cup of pulp.

❦   ❦

Pumpkins
in the Menu

MORNING COFFEE

Warm Pumpkin Bread*   Warm Orange Nut Bread**

Softened Butter

Pumpkin Jam*

Pumpkin Cake-Roll Slices*

Freshly Ground Hot Coffee   Cider

  *See Pumpkin Recipes
**See Orange Recipes

❦   ❦

Pumpkin Jam

1 5-pound pumpkin
2½ pounds sugar
3 cups (1 lb.) dried apricots, cut into strips
3 cups (1 lb.) raisins

Pare pumpkin. Remove seeds and cut pulp into cubes. In a bowl, combine pumpkin and sugar. Stir well, and allow to stand overnight. In the morning, cook slowly, stirring frequently, until pumpkin is tender and clear. Puree pumpkin mixture, add apricots and raisins, and cook until fruits are tender. Pour boiling hot mixture into sterile canning jars and seal, following manufacturer's directions.

Pumpkin Bread

2 eggs
½ cup (6 fl. oz.) honey
1 cup (8 oz.) pumpkin, cooked and pureed
½ cup (4 fl. oz.) vegetable oil
1 teaspoon baking soda
¼ cup (2 fl. oz.) buttermilk or yogurt
2 cups (10 oz.) whole wheat flour
½ teaspoon nutmeg
½ teaspoon cloves
½ teaspoon cinnamon

Preheat oven to 325° F. (165° C.).

Beat together eggs and honey. Add pumpkin and oil and mix well. In a small bowl, dissolve baking soda in buttermilk or yogurt. Sift together flour, nutmeg, cloves, and cinnamon and add to pumpkin mixture alternately with soda mixture. Pour batter into a greased 9 by 5 inch (23 by 13 cm.) loaf pan and bake for 1½ hours.

Pumpkin and Pork Chop Casserole

1 3-pound pumpkin, pared and coarsely chopped
¼ cup (1¾ oz.) brown sugar
¼ teaspoon pumpkin spice
¼ teaspoon mace
¼ teaspoon cinnamon
¼ teaspoon nutmeg
¼ cup (2 fl. oz.) water
2 tablespoons molasses
1 tablespoon butter
4 pork chops
salt and pepper, to taste

Preheat oven to 325° F. (165° C.).

In an oblong casserole dish arrange pumpkin. Sprinkle pumpkin with brown sugar, pumpkin spice, mace, cinnamon, nutmeg, water, and molasses. Set aside. Melt butter in a frying pan and brown pork chops. Arrange chops in casserole over pumpkin. Season with salt and pepper. Bake for 45 minutes, or until pork is tender.

Pumpkin-Shell Dessert

1 3-pound pumpkin
2 cups (12 oz.) apples, peeled, cored and chopped
1 cup (4 oz.) pecans, chopped
1 cup (5 oz.) raisins
⅓ to ½ cup (2¼ to 3½ oz.) sugar
1 teaspoon lemon juice
¼ teaspoon cinnamon
¼ teaspoon nutmeg
1 cup (8 fl. oz.) heavy cream

Preheat oven to 350° F. (180° C.).

Wash and dry pumpkin. Slice off top for lid, scrape out seeds and set lid aside. Fill pumpkin with apples, pecans, and raisins. Add sugar, lemon juice, cinnamon, and nutmeg. Mix well. Replace lid on pumpkin. Place on cookie sheet and bake until apples are tender, about 40 minutes.

To serve, spoon filling and some pumpkin from the shell into each serving dish. Whip cream and spoon over each portion.

Orange Pumpkin Custard Pie

8 eggs, separated
1½ cups (12 oz.) pumpkin, cooked and mashed
1 teaspoon salt
½ teaspoon cinnamon
pinch ginger
peel of one orange, grated
1½ cups (10½ oz.) sugar
½ cup (4 fl. oz.) orange juice
2 tablespoons butter, melted
2 cups (16 fl. oz.) milk
1 cup (8 fl. oz.) heavy cream
2 9-inch (23 cm.) pie shells, unbaked

Preheat oven to 400° F. (205° C.).

Beat egg yolks until light. Add pumpkin, salt, cinnamon, ginger, orange peel, sugar, orange juice, and melted butter. Mix well. Stir in milk and cream. Beat egg whites until stiff and fold into pumpkin mixture. Pour into pie shells. Bake in 400° F. (205° C.) oven for 15 minutes, then reduce heat to 350° F. (180° C.) and bake for 40 to 50 minutes, or until a knife inserted near the center comes out clean.

Pumpkin Cake Roll

Cake:

3 eggs
1 cup (7 oz.) sugar
⅔ cup (6 oz.) pumpkin, cooked and mashed
1 teaspoon lemon juice
¾ cup (3½ oz.) all-purpose flour
1 teaspoon baking powder
2 teaspoons cinnamon
1 teaspoon ginger
½ teaspoon nutmeg
½ teaspoon salt
1 cup (4 oz.) walnuts, chopped
powdered sugar, as needed

Preheat oven to 375° F. (190° C.).

Beat eggs at high speed for 5 minutes. Beat in sugar. Add pumpkin and lemon juice. Mix together flour, baking powder, cinnamon, ginger, nutmeg, and salt. Fold into egg mixture until combined. Pour into a 15 by 10 by 1 inch (38.5 by 25 by 2.5 cm.) jelly roll pan which has been greased, lined with waxed paper, and greased again. Top with walnuts. Bake for 15 minutes. Turn the cake out into a towel. Sprinkle with powdered sugar, roll up, and let cool.

Filling:

1 cup (5 oz.) powdered sugar
⅔ cup (6 oz.) cream cheese
4 tablespoons butter
½ teaspoon vanilla

Beat together powdered sugar, cream cheese, butter and vanilla. Unroll cake and spread filling evenly. Reroll cake, sprinkle with more powdered sugar, and chill. Serve cake at room temperature for the best flavor.

Pumpkin Chiffon Pie

1½ cups (12 oz.) pumpkin, cooked and mashed
3 egg yolks, beaten
¾ cup (5 oz.) brown sugar
½ teaspoon salt
1 teaspoon cinnamon
½ teaspoon nutmeg
½ cup (4 fl. oz.) milk
1 envelope unflavored gelatin
¼ cup (2 fl. oz.) cold water
3 egg whites
¼ cup (1¾ oz.) sugar
1 9-inch (23-cm.) pie shell, cooked and cooled
1 cup (8 fl. oz.) heavy cream

In a double boiler, combine pumpkin, egg yolks, brown sugar, salt, cinnamon, nutmeg, and milk. Cook over hot water until thickened. Remove from heat. In a bowl, combine gelatin and water and stir until smooth. Stir into pumpkin mixture. Chill until partially set. Beat egg whites slightly. Add sugar and beat until stiff peaks form. Fold into gelatin mixture. Pour filling into pie shell and chill until firm.

To serve, whip cream and use as a garnish.

Pumpkin Ice Cream Pie

1 8- or 9-ounce box ginger snaps
1 cup (8 oz.) pumpkin, cooked and mashed
¼ cup (1¾ oz.) brown sugar
½ teaspoon salt
½ teaspoon cinnamon
¼ teaspoon nutmeg
1 teaspoon ground cloves
½ teaspoon allspice
1 tablespoon bourbon
½ cup (2 oz.) pecans, chopped
1 quart vanilla ice cream, softened

Line the bottom and sides of a 9-inch (23-cm.) pie plate with whole ginger snaps. Set aside.

In a bowl, combine pumpkin, brown sugar, salt, cinnamon, nutmeg, cloves, allspice, bourbon, and pecans. Mix well and fold into ice cream.

To assemble pie, pour half the ice cream mixture into the prepared pie plate. Cover with a layer of ginger snaps. Add remaining ice cream and freeze until firm.

13 | RICE
Legend's Perfect Food

The Hindu god Shiva, legend says, hungered for the fa-
vors of the beautiful goddess Ratna Dumila, but she was
adamant in refusing him unless he could provide her
with her heart's desire: an absolutely perfect food. Poor
Shiva tried and tried, but Ratna Dumila would not be
satisfied and went to her death a virgin. From her tomb
sprouted the perfect food, too late for her and Shiva, but
in plenty of time for us: rice.

This legend gives us a clue to the importance of rice in
some countries. In Japan, rice fields mean so much to a
family that they are named, like relatives, and one polite
greeting used in the countryside as an equivalent to
"How are you?" is "Have you eaten your rice?"

When Japanese see pictures of rice being thrown at an American wedding, they are aghast: not one grain of rice should ever be wasted.

In some parts of China, the phrase "breaking bread" doesn't exist, but a phrase that means "eating rice" is used in the same way.

The Japanese say that rice has a soul and must be treated with respect. Natives of Borneo associate virility with rice consumption and caution visitors that they won't be *kuat*—able to produce sons and daughters—if they don't eat three large bowls of rice a day. All over the Orient, rice planting and rice harvest are times of jubilant celebration.

Rice is the staple food of 61 percent of the world's population, and in some countries, the average person eats four hundred pounds of rice a year. But a North American, who eats only about eight pounds annually, may not be eating enough of a good thing. Nutritionally, rice is rated "excellent" in protein quality, has a negligible fat content, and is a powerhouse of essential amino acids and minerals. Its low sodium content makes it a good bet for people on salt-restricted diets.

Don't be alarmed by all the different kinds of rice you will find on the supermarket shelves. California produces almost 20 percent of the United States output, primarily the pearl or medium-grain varieties. Texas, Arkansas, and Louisiana together produce the remaining 80 percent, mainly long-grained rice. Brown rice and white rice are the same varieties; the difference is that in brown rice the bran layer has not been milled off. Converted or parboiled rice is long-grain rice that has been specially processed to retain vitamins. Wild rice, surprisingly perhaps, is an aquatic grass seed and not rice at all.

Once you decide on a variety of rice and bring it home, it will keep indefinitely in a closed container in a cool, dry place.

To cook rice correctly, you should be aware of the distinction between pearl or medium-grain rice and the long-grain varieties. Unless you think gummy is yummy, the ideal proportion of water to rice for pearl or medium-grain white rice is one cup rice to one and one-half cups water and one teaspoon salt. One cup of long-grain rice will use two cups of water. Once the rice has simmered in a covered pan for about twenty minutes it should rest off the heat for another ten minutes or so—"long enough for cook and spouse to finish having a cocktail together," in the words of one grower.

The rule is a bit different for brown rice, preferred by many rice farmers for its nutlike flavor and richer concentration of nutrients. Use two cups of water for each cup of rice and simmer, covered, for about one hour. Cook converted rice according to package directions.

It is easy to tell when rice is done. Mash a cooked grain with a spoon. It should be equally tender all the way through, with no hard center or core. Also, it should have the same shape as the uncooked grain, only puffed and swollen. When overcooked, the rice grain changes shape, and not only becomes pasty but also it loses flavor.

Overcooking can be avoided, though, if you more or less follow directions. Rice farmers say that if you can boil water, you can cook rice. And don't worry, it's not a stopwatch kind of business. "After all," points out California rice farmer's wife Carole Southam, "billions of people cooked this kind of rice and got it right for at least five thousand years before watches were ever imagined."

❦ ❧

Rice
in the Menu

DINNER FOR TWO

California Colombard

Cream of Rice Soup*

Paella Salad*

Crusty French Bread and Butter

Caramel Rice Custard*

Coffee or Tea   Liqueur or Cognac

*See Rice Recipes

❧ ❦

Cream of Rice Soup

½ cup (4 oz.) rice
¼ cup (1½ oz.) onion, chopped
4 cups (32 fl. oz.) chicken or beef stock
1 teaspoon salt
½ teaspoon pepper
1 cup (8 fl. oz.) heavy cream, heated
2 egg yolks
1 cup (5 oz.) croutons

Combine rice, onion, and stock. Bring to a boil and simmer 45 minutes, or until rice is tender. Add salt and pepper. Combine cream and egg yolks. Add a small amount of hot soup liquid, then pour cream mixture into soup. Stir until thickened. Add croutons and serve at once.

Lace-Edge Rice Breakfast Cakes

2 eggs, separated
1 cup (8 fl. oz.) milk
¼ teaspoon salt
½ cup (2½ oz.) all-purpose flour
½ cup (1½ oz.) cooked rice
2 tablespoons butter, melted
1 teaspoon butter
powdered sugar, as needed

Beat egg whites until stiff. Set aside. Beat yolks until light and thick. Add milk, salt, and flour to yolks and beat until smooth. Stir in rice and melted butter. Fold in egg whites. Heat 1 teaspoon butter in frying pan and fry cakes, turning once. Serve with powdered sugar.

Brown-Rice Raisin Bread

1⅔ cups (13⅓ fl. oz.) water
1 cup (8 oz.) short-grain brown rice
1 tablespoon butter
½ teaspoon salt
2 packages active dry yeast
2 cups (16 fl. oz.) warm water, 105°–115° F.
(41°– 46° C.)
3 cups (15 oz.) whole wheat flour
⅓ cup (4 fl. oz.) honey
¼ cup (2 fl. oz.) vegetable oil
2 teaspoons salt
1½ cups (8 oz.) raisins
4 to 5 cups (20 to 25 oz.) all-purpose flour

In a medium saucepan, combine the 1⅔ cups water, rice, butter, and the ½ teaspoon salt. Bring to a rolling boil. Reduce heat to low, cover and simmer for 30 to 35 minutes, or until all liquid is absorbed. Remove from heat (do not stir rice) and let stand, covered, for 10 minutes. Uncover and allow cooked rice to cool to lukewarm.

Dissolve yeast in ½ cup (4 fl. oz.) of the warm water. Add cooked rice, whole wheat flour, remaining 1½ cups (12 fl. oz.) warm water, honey, oil, and the 2 teaspoons salt. Beat until smooth. Stir in raisins and enough all-purpose flour to make a stiff dough. Turn onto a lightly floured surface. Knead until smooth and elastic, 10 to 20 minutes, adding more all-purpose flour if necessary. Place dough in greased bowl; turn greased side up. Cover dough and let rise in warm place until it doubles in size (about 1 hour).

Punch dough down and divide it in half. Roll each half into a 12 by 8 inch (30 by 20 cm.) rectangle. Roll up tightly from narrow end, sealing as you roll. Seal edges; fold under. Place each loaf in a greased 9 by 5 inch (23 by 13 cm.) loaf pan. Cover and let dough rise in warm place until double in size (about 1½ hours).

Preheat oven to 375° F. (190° C.). Bake for 35 to 45 minutes, or until bread sounds hollow when tapped with finger. Immediately remove from pans. Cool.

Savory Rice, Broccoli, and Cheese Bake

1 cup (8 oz.) medium-grain rice
1½ cups (12 fl. oz.) water
1 tablespoon butter
½ teaspoon salt
¼ cup (2 fl. oz.) butter
¼ cup (1½ oz.) onion, finely chopped
1 clove garlic, minced
1½ pounds broccoli, cooked and chopped
½ cup (3 oz.) Monterey Jack or other mild cheese
4 eggs
½ cup (4 fl. oz.) milk
1 teaspoon salt
¼ teaspoon pepper
1¼ teaspoons thyme
½ cup (3 oz.) Cheddar cheese

Preheat oven to 350° F. (180° C.).

In a saucepan, combine rice, water, 1 tablespoon butter, and salt. Bring to a rolling boil. Reduce heat to low, cover, and simmer for 12 to 15 minutes. Remove from heat (do not stir rice) and let stand, covered, for 10 minutes. Meanwhile, melt ¼ cup (2 fl. oz.) butter in a pan. Add onion and garlic and sauté until tender. Combine rice, onion mixture, broccoli, and Monterey Jack cheese; mix well.

In a bowl, combine eggs, milk, 1 teaspoon salt, pepper, and thyme; mix well. Stir into rice mixture. Turn into buttered 8-inch (20-cm.) square baking dish. Sprinkle with Cheddar cheese. Bake for 20 to 25 minutes, or until set.

Zucchini Quiche in Brown Rice Crust

Crust:

  1⅔ cups (13⅓ fl. oz.) water
  1 cup (8 oz.) brown rice
  1 tablespoon butter
  ½ teaspoon salt
  1 egg, beaten

Combine water, rice, butter, and salt in medium saucepan. Bring to a rolling boil. Reduce heat to low, cover, and simmer 30 to 35 minutes, or until all liquid is absorbed. Remove from heat (do not stir rice) and let stand, covered, for 10 minutes. Remove cover and allow to cool. Stir egg into cooled rice; mix well. Press onto bottom and sides of a 10-inch (25-cm.) greased pie plate. Set aside.

Filling:

  2 tablespoons butter
  1¼ cups (8 oz.) zucchini, sliced
  ⅔ cup (4 oz.) onion, chopped
  1¼ cups (4 oz.) mushrooms, sliced
  ¾ cup (4½ oz.) Cheddar cheese, grated
  1 cup (8 fl. oz.) milk
  3 eggs
  ¼ teaspoon salt
  dash cayenne pepper
  dash nutmeg
  paprika, as needed

Preheat oven to 325° F. (165° C.).
  Melt 1 tablespoon of the butter in a skillet. Add zucchini and cook until crisp-tender, about 5 minutes. Remove zucchini, set aside. Melt remaining 1 tablespoon butter in same skillet. Add onion, cook until crisp-tender, about 3 minutes. Add mushrooms, and cook 2 to 3 minutes.

Spread onions and mushrooms over rice. Sprinkle with cheese and top with zucchini. Beat milk, eggs, salt, cayenne pepper, and nutmeg together. Pour over zucchini. Sprinkle with paprika. Cover rim of pie plate with foil. Bake for 45 to 55 minutes, or until set.

California Rice Torta

4 cups (11 oz.) cooked rice
4 eggs, beaten
⅔ cup (5 oz.) cooked onions
⅔ cup (5 oz.) cooked spinach
1 cup (8 fl. oz.) olive oil
1¼ cups (5 oz.) Parmesan cheese, grated
⅓ teaspoon garlic powder
⅓ teaspoon thyme
⅜ teaspoon dry basil
salt and pepper, to taste
1 egg white, slightly beaten

Preheat oven to 375° F. (190° C.).

Rub a 9 by 13 inch (23 by 33 cm.) baking pan with olive oil. Set aside. Combine rice, eggs, onions, spinach, olive oil, 1 cup (6 oz.) of the Parmesan cheese, garlic powder, thyme, basil, salt, and pepper. Mix well and spread evenly in oiled baking pan.

Heat egg white and pour over rice mixture. Sprinkle with remaining ¼ cup (1 oz.) Parmesan cheese. Bake for 45 minutes, or until set. To serve, cut into squares.

Crunchy Rice Salad

Salad:

    3 cups (8 oz.) cooked rice, cooled
    3 cups (24 oz.) cooked turkey or chicken, diced
    1 cup (6 oz.) celery, sliced
    1 cup (6 oz.) green pepper, chopped
    1 cup (7 oz.) water chestnuts, sliced

Gently combine rice, turkey or chicken, celery, green pepper, and water chestnuts.

Dressing:

    ¾ cup (6 oz.) mayonnaise
    1 teaspoon lemon peel, grated
    ¼ cup (2 fl. oz.) lemon juice
    1 tablespoon horseradish
    1 tablespoon mustard
    ¼ teaspoon garlic powder
    ½ cup (3 oz.) green onions, thinly sliced
    ¼ cup (1 oz.) parsley, chopped
    ⅓ cup (2 oz.) pimientos, chopped
    salt and pepper, to taste

Garnish:

    ½ cup (4 oz.) almonds, toasted and sliced

Blend together mayonnaise, lemon peel, lemon juice, horseradish, mustard, and garlic powder. Stir in green onions, parsley, and pimiento. Add salt and pepper. Pour dressing over salad. Mix well, cover, and chill at least 4 hours.

To serve, garnish with almonds.

Paella Salad

6 ounces shrimp, cooked
2 cups (6 oz.). rice, cooked and cooled
1 cup (8 oz.) chicken, cooked and diced
1 cup (6 oz.) celery, sliced
1 cup (6 oz.) peas, cooked
⅓ cup (2 oz.) green pepper, diced
¼ cup (1½ oz.) green onions, sliced
⅔ cup (6 fl. oz.) mayonnaise
2 tablespoons dry white wine
¼ teaspoon salt
pinch garlic powder
¼ teaspoon freshly ground pepper
2 tomatoes, cut in wedges

Combine shrimp, rice, chicken, celery, peas, green pepper, and onions. In a small bowl, blend mayonnaise with wine, salt, garlic powder, and pepper. Pour dressing over shrimp mixture and toss lightly. Chill at least 1 hour and garnish with tomatoes.

Skillet Tostada Dinner

1 pound ground beef
1 onion, finely chopped
1 clove garlic, minced
1 tablespoon chili powder
1 tablespoon all-purpose flour
½ cup (4 fl. oz.) water
2 tomatoes, seeded and chopped
1½ cups (4 oz.) dark red kidney beans, cooked
salt and pepper, to taste
1 cup (8 oz.) medium-grain rice
1½ cups (12 fl. oz.) hot and spicy vegetable juice
2 tablespoons water
1 tablespoon butter
⅛ teaspoon salt
1 cup (8 fl. oz.) sour cream
1 cup (6 oz.) Cheddar cheese, shredded
1 avocado, peeled and sliced

In a large skillet, brown meat, onion, and garlic; drain. Combine chili powder and flour; sprinkle over meat. Stir in ½ cup (4 fl. oz.) water. Simmer 10 minutes, stirring occasionally. Stir in tomatoes, beans, salt, and pepper. Simmer 5 minutes longer. Remove mixture from skillet, cover, and keep warm. Wipe out skillet.

Rinse rice with cold water until water runs clear; drain well. In the same skillet used for meat mixture, combine rice, vegetable juice, 2 tablespoons water, butter, and ⅛ teaspoon salt. Bring to a boil; stir. Reduce heat to low, cover, and simmer 15 to 20 minutes until liquid is absorbed and rice is tender. Remove from heat and let stand, covered, for 5 minutes; then fluff with a fork.

To serve, spoon meat mixture over rice. Top with sour cream, cheese, and avocado slices.

Caramel Rice Custard

12 caramels
4 teaspoons water
8 to 10 pecan halves, toasted
2 cups (16 fl. oz.) milk
1⅓ cups (10⅔ fl. oz.) water
1 cup (8 oz.) medium-grain rice
⅓ cup (2¼ oz.) sugar
1 tablespoon butter
½ teaspoon nutmeg
½ teaspoon salt
3 eggs, beaten
1½ tablespoons cream sherry
1½ teaspoons vanilla
1 cup (8 fl. oz.) heavy cream

Preheat oven to 350° F. (180° C.).

In top of double boiler over hot water, melt caramels in 4 teaspoons water. Spread melted caramels on bottom and sides of a 6-cup (48-oz.) ring mold. Arrange nut halves on bottom. Set aside.

In a saucepan, combine milk, 1⅓ cups (10⅔ fl. oz.) water, rice, sugar, butter, nutmeg, and salt. Bring to a rolling boil. Stir well. Reduce heat to low, cover, and simmer for 15 to 20 minutes, or until rice is tender. Remove from heat. Let stand, covered, 10 minutes. Stir well. In a bowl, gradually stir 1 cup (3 oz.) of the rice mixture into eggs. Pour back into saucepan, mixing with the rest of the rice mixture. Add sherry and vanilla; mix well. Pour mixture into mold. Bake for 20 to 25 minutes, or until set. Run knife around edges of mold. Immediately invert onto serving plate. Let mold remain 3 to 4 minutes; remove.

Serve warm with cream, whipped, as a garnish.

14 | TOMATOES
Our Most Popular Berries

Next time you're carefully slicing a large, fresh, vine-ripened tomato into your salad bowl, ponder the following fact: that is not a vegetable you're dealing with. In fact, it's a fruit, and not just a fruit, but a berry. Botanically speaking, the flesh that surrounds the seed of any plant is a fruit, and if those seeds are scattered around, rather than located in a central core or pit, that fruit is a berry.

Tomato growers have a particular reason to be proud of the "berry" they grow. Tomatoes provide us with more of the ten most important vitamins and minerals than any of the other top ten fruits and vegetables consumed in the United States. Curiously, this isn't because they have a particularly high nutritional value. Tomatoes are actually exceeded in vitamin and mineral content by quite a few vegetables, including broccoli, spinach, brussel sprouts, and lima beans. These vegetables all outrank tomatoes for concentration of vitamins and minerals. The reason tomatoes top the list as a provider of nutrients is that we eat so much of them.

In fact, the average man, woman, and child in the United States eats more than sixty pounds of tomatoes a year. Much of this amount is consumed in the form of spaghetti sauce or pizzas or tomato ketchup or Bloody Marys.

Tomatoes are just about a dietary staple for us today, but as recently as the turn of the century, Americans ate less than a pound of tomatoes per person in the course of a year. People knew that tomatoes belong to the deadly nightshade family, and assumed that they also were poisonous. Of course, they couldn't have been more wrong. In fact, Dr. Charles Rick, of the University of California at Davis, enjoys telling the story of Richard L. Graves, the Tomato Man of the East, who for years has lived on nothing but tomatoes. Graves eats twenty pounds of them a day and nothing else. Dr. Rick was puzzled by this, but after consulting with colleagues at the University of California Medical School, he concluded that it would be possible for a not very active, elderly person to meet all his dietary requirements with tomatoes alone. Although this is theoretically possible, Dr. Rick is emphatic about not recommending such a diet.

When tomatoes are part of a balanced diet, with foods selected from the four major food groups, they do play an important part in nutrition. One average-size tomato contains only 27 calories, yet contributes more than 1000 International Units of vitamin A (about one-fifth of the Recommended Daily Allowance), and 28 milligrams of ascorbic acid, or about one-half of the RDA for vitamin C.

How should tomatoes be purchased and stored to insure maximum nutrition and flavor? At the supermarket, for fruit to use within three days, look for red, ripe, unbruised tomatoes. Select pink tomatoes for use within three to six days and set them stem up for ripening. Dr. Charles Rick says the most important thing we should know about storing tomatoes is, "Do not refrigerate them!" Tomatoes are tropical fruits, and chilling them causes a rapid breakdown of texture, flavor, resistance to mold, and destruction of vitamin C.

"We discovered this," Rick tells us, "when refrigerated box cars first began shipping farm products back East. Suddenly we were deluged with complaints about the quality of our tomatoes. Customers who had always been satisfied before were suddenly complaining that the flavor was no good, the texture mushy, and the tomatoes went bad sooner than ever before." University experts found that the chilling temperatures were causing the problem.

Room temperature is ideal for tomatoes. Avoid direct sunlight or temperatures over 75 degrees Fahrenheit (24 degrees Celsius), since this tends to make the tomatoes flavorless and mushy—and who wants to ruin such a good thing?

Tomatoes
in the Menu

BUFFET SUPPER

Cold Beer   Red Wine

Fresh Tomato Salsa Appetizer*

with Corn Tortilla Chips

Cream of Fresh Pea Soup**

Garden Salad with Poppy Seed Dressing*

Tomato Zucchini Parmesan*

Fresh Tomato Pizza*

Ice Cream

Coffee or Tea

*See Tomato Recipes
**See Milk Recipes

Tomato-Avocado Pita Sandwiches

5 medium tomatoes, sliced
¼ cup (2 fl. oz.) vegetable oil
2 tablespoons red wine vinegar
½ teaspoon basil, crushed
¼ teaspoon salt
⅛ teaspoon pepper
2 avocados, peeled, pitted, and mashed
3 tablespoons green chili, diced
2 tablespoons mayonnaise
2 teaspoons lemon juice
1 teaspoon onion, minced
½ teaspoon garlic salt
6 pita breads, halved
1 cup (3 oz.) alfalfa or bean sprouts
¼ cup (1½ oz.) green onion, sliced
¾ cup (4½ oz.) Monterey Jack or mild Cheddar
    cheese, grated

Place tomato slices in a shallow dish. Combine oil, vinegar, basil, salt, and pepper in a jar with a tight-fitting lid. Cover and shake well; pour over tomatoes. Cover tomatoes and let stand at room temperature for 1 hour. Combine avocado, chili, mayonnaise, lemon juice, onion, and garlic salt; blend well. Cover and chill.

To serve, spread inside of each pita bread half with 2 tablespoons of the avocado mixture. Spoon in about 1 tablespoon sprouts. Add 2 to 3 tomato slices, 1 teaspoon green onion, and 1 tablespoon cheese.

Fresh Tomato Salsa Appetizer

4 to 5 tomatoes, peeled, cored, and chopped
4 tablespoons onion, finely chopped
1 tablespoon fresh oregano
½ clove garlic, finely chopped
1 teaspoon salt, or more to taste
dash crushed chili pepper, or more to taste
dash pepper

In a blender, combine tomatoes, onion, oregano, garlic, salt, chili pepper, and pepper. Blend at low speed for 10 to 20 seconds.

Serve with tortilla chips or deep-fried tortillas for scooping the dip.

Fresh Tomato Summer Salad

1 sweet red onion, sliced in circles
2 tomatoes, sliced
1 bell pepper, sliced
salt and pepper, to taste
2 tablespoons red wine vinegar
6 tablespoons olive oil

On a large platter, alternately layer onion, tomato, and bell pepper slices. Season with salt and pepper, and pour vinegar and oil over all. Allow vegetables to sit at room temperature for 1 hour; then chill.

Garden Salad with Poppy Seed Dressing

Salad:

 3 medium tomatoes, cored and cut into wedges
 2 carrots, sliced
 1¼ cups (4 oz.) mushrooms, sliced
 ½ cucumber, sliced
 ⅓ cup (2⅔ oz.) green onion, sliced
 5 cups (24 oz.) lettuce, torn

Combine tomatoes, carrots, mushrooms, cucumber, green onion, and lettuce in a salad bowl. Set aside.

Dressing:

 ½ cup (4 fl. oz.) apple cider vinegar
 ½ cup (4 fl. oz.) vegetable oil
 2 teaspoons poppy seeds
 2 teaspoons Dijon mustard
 2 teaspoons honey
 ¼ teaspoon onion salt
 ⅛ teaspoon paprika

Combine vinegar, oil, poppy seeds, mustard, honey, onion salt, and paprika in a jar with a tight-fitting lid. Cover and shake well. Chill.

To serve, pour poppy seed dressing over fresh vegetables and toss.

Shrimp and Tomatoes with Savory Rice

1 cup (8 oz.) medium-grain rice
1½ cups (12 fl. oz.) chicken stock
3 tablespoons butter
1 bay leaf
¾ teaspoon salt
¼ teaspoon tarragon, crushed
⅛ teaspoon paprika
½ cup (3 oz.) onion, chopped
1 clove garlic, minced
1⅓ cups (4 oz.) mushrooms, sliced
1½ pounds medium shrimp or prawns, cooked and deveined
6 to 8 artichoke hearts, cooked and quartered (optional)
4 tomatoes, cut in wedges
2 tablespoons lemon juice
¼ cup (1 oz.) parsley, chopped

Combine rice, stock, 1 tablespoon of the butter, bay leaf, salt, tarragon, and paprika in a medium saucepan. Bring to a rolling boil. Reduce heat to low, cover, and simmer 15 to 20 minutes, or until all liquid is absorbed. Remove from heat. Let stand, covered, 10 minutes. Meanwhile, melt remaining 2 tablespoons butter in a large skillet. Add onion and garlic, and cook until almost tender. Add mushrooms, and cook for 1 to 2 minutes. Stir in shrimp, artichoke hearts (if used), and tomatoes. Heat through. Drain. Remove bay leaf from rice and fluff rice with fork. Stir rice, lemon juice, and parsley into shrimp mixture.

Pesto-Stuffed Tomatoes

8 tomatoes (about 2¾ lb.)
1¼ cups (10 oz.) peas
¾ cup (3 oz.) Parmesan cheese, grated
⅓ cup (2⅔ fl. oz.) butter, melted
¼ cup (1 oz.) packed parsley sprigs
1 tablespoon dried basil, crushed
1 clove garlic, sliced
¼ cup (1 oz.) walnuts, finely chopped

Preheat oven to 350° F. (180° C.).

Core tomatoes. Scoop out inside. Chop pulp and set aside; discard seeds. Turn tomato shells upside down on a paper towel to drain. Combine peas, Parmesan cheese, butter, parsley, basil, and garlic in a food processor or blender container. Cover and blend until smooth. Fold in chopped tomato pulp and walnuts. Place tomato shells in shallow baking pan. Spoon pea mixture into shells. Sprinkle with additional Parmesan cheese, if desired. Bake for 20 to 25 minutes.

Tomatoes and Peas in Mustard Dill Sauce

2 tomatoes, cored and cut into wedges
1¼ cups (10 oz.) peas, cooked
½ cup (4 fl. oz.) sour ceam
1¼ teaspoons Dijon mustard
½ teaspoon dill, crushed
dash pepper

In a bowl, combine tomatoes, peas, sour cream, mustard, dill, and pepper. Cook in a saucepan over low heat until heated through.

Fresh Tomato Pizza

Sauce:

olive oil, as needed
2 cloves garlic, finely minced
2 onions, finely minced
16 cups (8 lbs.) tomatoes, peeled and whirled in
   the blender until creamy
2 teaspoons oregano, or more to taste

Dough:

1 package dry yeast
1 cup (8 fl. oz.) water, warmed
3 cups (15 oz.) all-purpose flour
1 tablespoon olive oil
1 teaspoon salt

Topping:

3 cups (18 oz.) Italian cheese, grated (use a variety
   of Italian cheeses)
4 tomatoes, sliced

To prepare sauce, pour a thin layer of olive oil onto the bottom of a large, deep pot. Add garlic and onion and cook until light brown. Add tomatoes and cook until mixture reaches a light, rolling boil. Add oregano, lower heat, and simmer for at least 2 hours, stirring often until thick.

To prepare dough, dissolve yeast in warm water. Add flour, olive oil, and salt. On a floured board, knead until dough is soft. Place in a greased bowl, cover with a towel, and allow to rise in a warm place until doubled, about 1 hour. Punch dough down, divide into two balls, and spread each onto a 12-inch (30-cm.) round pan. Allow dough to rise again for 30 minutes, or until puffed.

Preheat oven to 400° F. (205° C.).

To cook, spread sauce on prepared pizza dough, sprinkle with cheese, and bake for 25 to 30 minutes. Remove pizza from oven and top with tomatoes. Serve immediately.

Fresh Tomato Sauce and Red Pasta

Sauce:

> olive oil, as needed
> 2 onions, finely chopped
> 2 cloves garlic, finely chopped
> 1 cup (8 oz.) finely chopped chicken giblets
> 1 cup (8 oz.) finely ground pork
> 1 cup (8 oz.) extra-lean ground beef
> 1 cup (8 oz.) ground veal
> pork, beef, and veal bones, if available
> 16 cups (8 lbs.) tomatoes, peeled and whirled in a
>   blender or processor until creamy
> 1 cup (8 fl. oz.) red wine
> salt and pepper, to taste
> Italian herbs, to taste

Pour a very thin layer of olive oil onto the bottom of a large, deep pot. Add onions and garlic and sauté until nut-brown. Add giblets, pork, beef, veal, and meat bones, if available. Brown well and stir often over medium-low heat. Meanwhile, prepare tomatoes. When all fat is rendered from the meat, add tomatoes, wine, salt, pepper, and herbs. Let mixture sit for 10 minutes; then cook on lowest heat for 5 to 8 hours, stirring occasionally. When fully cooked the sauce will be rusty-red color. Remove meat bones, if used.

Pasta:

> 3 cups (15 oz.) all-purpose flour
> 4 eggs
> 2 teaspoons water, if needed
> ½ cup (4 oz.) tomatoes, cooked and pureed

Combine flour and eggs and work into a ball. Gradually add tomato puree. Knead dough until soft and no longer sticky. Divide dough in half. Using a long rolling pin and a well-floured board, roll dough very thin to form an 18-inch (45-cm.) round. Roll up and slice into ½-inch (1½-cm.) strips. Repeat with remaining ball of dough. Bring a large pot of water to boil, add strips of pasta, and boil until tender.

Topping:

2 cups (12 oz.) cheese, grated (use a variety of Italian cheeses)

To serve, top pasta with sauce and sprinkle with cheese.

Tomato Zucchini Parmesan

1 cup (8 fl. oz.) tomato sauce
¾ cup (6 oz). tomato paste
¾ cup (4½ oz.) onion, finely chopped
2 teaspoons Italian herb seasoning
1 clove garlic, minced
¼ teaspoon salt
4 cups (1½ lb.) zucchini, sliced ¼-inch (¾-cm.) thick
4 tomatoes, cored and sliced
½ cup (2 oz.) Parmesan cheese, grated
8 ounces Monterey Jack or mild Cheddar cheese, sliced

Preheat oven to 375° F. (190 ° C.).

In a medium saucepan, combine tomato sauce, tomato paste, onion, Italian herb seasoning, garlic, and salt. Bring mixture to a boil. Reduce heat, simmer 15 minutes, stirring occasionally. In a 9 by 13 inch (23 by 33 cm.) pan, layer half of the zucchini, tomatoes, sauce, and Parmesan cheese. Repeat layers. Place Monterey Jack or mild Cheddar cheese on top. Cover with aluminum foil. Bake for 40 to 45 minutes, or until zucchini is tender.

SECTION
3

NUTS AND
HONEY

15 | ALMONDS
*The Nuts That
Really Aren't*

You've just eaten a couple of hickory-smoked, roasted almonds and you're reaching for another, anticipating its salty crunchiness.

Pssst! You! Did you know you're not eating a nut—but a fruit kernel? In fact, almonds are so closely related to peaches that many almond trees are grafted onto peach rootstocks. As far as shape goes, you'd have to be an expert to tell their blossoms or developing fruits apart. It's only when the two fruits approach maturity that the peach's outer layer expands into the edible fruit we eat, while the almond's outer layer turns into its leatherlike hull. That almond you were eating corresponds to the kernel inside a peach pit.

Almond growers are immensely proud of their unusual "fruit"—large overseas sales of almonds regularly contribute significantly and positively to our balance of payments. There's a good reason for these high export sales. Almonds have such demanding cultural requirements that they can only be grown commercially in California and a few countries near the Mediterranean. To flourish, almonds must have hot summer days, cool evenings, low humidity, and, in winter, several hundred hours of freezing or near-freezing weather. California offers just these conditions, and it does so more predictably than any other place in the world.

February, when California almond trees burst forth with their snow-colored blossoms, is a time of beauty for Californians and visitors alike—and a time of anxiety for the growers. Almond trees will bear only if their blossoms are cross-pollinated with trees of a different variety. "The trick," explains Trina Van Unen, a member of the California Almond Growers Exchange, "is to have the early blossoming soft-shelled varieties last long enough for bees to transfer pollen to the hard-shelled varieties, which won't bloom for another ten days."

An almond grower's worst fear is a blossom-destroying frost. To combat frost, modern orchards often have hundreds of miles of underground pipes serving thermostatically controlled sprinklers, which are activated at 32 degrees Fahrenheit (0 degrees Celsius). An ice coating at 32 degrees Fahrenheit is usually warmer than frost, and though it may seem paradoxical, blossoms can survive several hours of subfreezing temperatures when protected by this icy insulation.

Farmer's wife Gerda Faye likes to look at almond blossoms after the sprinklers have been turned on. "You come out in the morning, and there are millions of ice-covered blossoms, flashing in the sun like a forest of giant Fourth of July sparklers."

Climatic conditions together with progressive cultural practices mean California regularly gets higher almond yields and better quality than any other country. And since almonds can grow in so few places, they are a rare and prestigious item in many countries. In Japan, California's second largest market after Germany, an impressive gift to a hostess is neither flowers nor wine, as it might be in America. No, it's a couple of tins of California almonds.

Such a gift is a healthy one, too. Almonds contribute significantly to a balanced diet. They are low in cholesterol and high in linoleic acid—good for healthy, glowing skin—rich in phosphorus and magnesium, and a valuable source of iron, calcium, and riboflavin. Twenty kernels contain about 165 calories.

Almonds are easily stored. Just keep them in the refrigerator in a tightly sealed container and they'll stay fresh for several months.

❧ ❧

Almonds
in the Menu

DINNER

Smoked Cocktail Almonds   White or Red Wine

Almond Slaw*

Chenin Blanc

Almond Hawaiian Beef*

Hot Buttered Rice

Asparagus Sauté**

Almond Paste Bars*

Coffee or Tea   Almond Liqueur

*See Almond Recipes
**See Asparagus Recipes

❧ ❧

Almond Slaw

¼ cup (1 oz.) almonds, toasted and slivered
2 cups (12 oz.) cabbage, shredded
1 cup (8 oz.) pineapple, finely chopped
¼ cup (2 fl. oz.) light cream
1 teaspoon lemon juice
½ teaspoon salt
pepper, as desired

Combine almonds, cabbage, and pineapple. Stir together cream, lemon juice, salt, and pepper. Pour dressing over cabbage mixture and toss lightly.

Broccoli with Almond Sauce

4 tablespoons butter
2½ tablespoons all-purpose flour
1¼ cups (10 fl. oz.) milk
¼ teaspoon salt
dash cayenne pepper
2 egg yolks
2 tablespoons lemon juice
3 cups (1½ lb.) broccoli, cooked and hot
⅓ cup (1¼ oz.) almonds, toasted and slivered

Melt 2 tablespoons butter and blend in flour. Add milk, salt, and cayenne, and cook and stir until mixture boils and thickens. Beat egg yolks lightly. Stir a little of the hot sauce into yolks; then combine the yolks with remaining sauce. Cook and stir over low heat for 3 or 4 minutes longer, but do not allow mixture to boil. Stir in remaining butter, 1 tablespoon at a time. Slowly stir in lemon juice. Pour sauce over broccoli and sprinkle with almonds.

Almond Beef Hawaiian

½ teaspoon ginger
1 teaspoon sugar
2 teaspoons cornstarch
¼ cup (2 fl. oz.) soy sauce
½ cup (4 fl. oz.) water
3 tablespoons vegetable oil
1 pound beef sirloin, cut into thin strips
1 clove garlic, halved
1 medium onion, sliced
1 cup (6 oz.) celery, sliced
½ cup (4 oz.) green pepper, cubed
6 cherry tomatoes, halved
¾ cup (3 oz.) almonds, slivered and toasted
hot cooked rice, as needed

Combine ginger, sugar, cornstarch, soy sauce, and water; set aside. In a large, heavy skillet or wok, heat to very hot 2 tablespoons oil. Add about half the beef and garlic; brown quickly. Remove from skillet or wok and brown remaining beef and garlic the same way. Discard garlic; add remaining oil to pan. Stir in onion and celery and coat with oil, keeping pan very hot. Cover and cook for about 1 minute. Stir in soy sauce mixture; cook until thickened. Move vegetables to one side of skillet. Return meat to skillet; add green pepper, tomato, and ½ cup (2 oz.) almonds. Keep meat, celery mixture, and green pepper mixture separate, but spoon sauce over all. Cover and heat for 1 minute. Serve immediately, spooned over rice. Garnish with remaining almonds.

Puff-Up Fillets

1 pound fish fillets
2 tablespoons butter
2 tablespoons all-purpose flour
¼ teaspoon salt
dash cayenne pepper
1 cup (8 fl. oz.) milk
½ cup (4 oz.) mild cheese, grated
1 tablespoon sherry
1/3 cup (1¼ oz.) almonds, roasted and diced

Poach fish, in boiling salted water to cover, for 15 to 20 minutes, or until tender. Drain and place in shallow baking dish. Meanwhile, melt butter and blend in flour, salt, and cayenne pepper. Add milk and cook and stir until thickened. Blend in cheese and sherry, and stir over very low heat until cheese is melted. Pour sauce over poached fish, sprinkle with almonds, and place under broiler for 2 to 3 minutes until heated and bubbly.

Sole in Almond Shrimp Sauce

1 to 1½ pounds sole fillets
1 cup (8 fl. oz.) white wine
3 ounces shrimp, cooked and deveined
4 tablespoons (2 fl. oz.) butter
2 tablespoons all-purpose flour
½ cup (4 fl. oz.) half-and-half
¼ teaspoon salt
dash pepper
⅓ cup (1¼ oz.) almonds, toasted and slivered

Preheat oven to 350° F. (180° C.).

Place sole in a 9 by 13 inch (23 by 33 cm.) baking dish. Pour wine over fish and bake for 15 to 20 minutes.

Meanwhile set aside ¼ cup (1 oz.) shrimp. Mash remaining shrimp with 2 tablespoons of the butter. Set aside. When fish is cooked, remove to a heated platter. Measure ½ cup (4 fl. oz.) cooking liquid and reserve. In a small saucepan, heat remaining butter, add flour, and cook, while stirring, for 2 minutes. Slowly add half-and-half, stirring constantly. When thickened, add reserved fish liquid and cook until mixture comes to a boil. Reduce heat, add mashed shrimp mixture, salt, and pepper. Stir until shrimp is warmed through. Add ¼ cup (1 oz.) of the almonds. Drain liquid from sole, pour sauce over fish, and garnish with reserved shrimp and remaining almonds.

Almond Tea Cookies

¼ cup (2 oz.) shortening
¼ cup (2 fl. oz.) butter
¼ cup (1¾ oz.) brown sugar
1 egg, separated
1 teaspoon almond extract
¼ teaspoon salt
1 cup (5 oz.) all-purpose flour
½ cup (2 oz.) almonds, chopped

Preheat oven to 350° F. (180° C.).

Combine shortening, butter, brown sugar, egg yolk, almond extract, and salt. Mix thoroughly. Add flour and shape dough into round, walnut-sized balls. Dip balls into beaten egg white, then roll in almonds. Place on cookie sheet 1-inch apart. Bake for 15 minutes.

Almond Paste Bars

Pastry:

> ½ cup (4 fl. oz.) butter
> ½ cup (4 oz.) shortening
> ½ cup (3½ oz.) brown sugar
> ½ cup (3½ oz.) sugar
> 1 egg
> 2 cups (10 oz.) all-purpose flour
> ½ teaspoon baking powder
> ¼ teaspoon salt

Combine butter, shortening, sugars, egg, flour, baking powder, and salt in order given. Place half the dough into a 9 by 13 inch (23 by 35 cm.) pan and pat down. Reserve remaining dough.

Filling:

> 1¼ cups (5 oz.) whole blanched almonds
> 1¼ cups (6 oz.) powdered sugar
> 1 egg white
> 1 tablespoon almond extract
> ½ teaspoon salt
> ¾ cup (5 oz.) sugar
> 2 eggs

Preheat oven to 325° F. (165° C.). Grind almonds, a portion at a time, in a blender or food grinder. Add powdered sugar, egg white, almond extract, and salt. Work into a stiff paste. Add sugar and eggs and stir until smooth.

Place filling on dough in pan and cover with remaining dough. Bake for 45 minutes.

Topping:

> 1 cup (5 oz.) powdered sugar
> 2 tablespoons water

½ teaspoon butter
1 teaspoon almond extract
dash salt
¼ cup (1 oz.) almonds, slivered

Mix together powdered sugar, water, butter, almond extract, and salt. Spread topping over warm cake and sprinkle with almonds. When cool, cut cake into bars.

Dutch Almond Cookies

¾ cup (6 fl oz.) butter
½ cup (3½ oz.) sugar
1½ cups (7½ oz.) all-purpose flour
¼ teaspoon baking soda
¼ teaspoon salt
1 egg, beaten
½ cup (2 oz.) almonds, slivered

Preheat oven to 350° F. (180° C.).

Cream butter and sugar. Add flour, baking soda, and salt and mix well. On a floured board, roll out dough into a 12-inch (30-cm.) square. Cut dough into 2-inch (5-cm.) squares. Brush with egg and sprinkle with almonds. Place on baking sheet and bake cookies about 8 minutes, or until light brown.

Almond Chocolate Soufflé

3 tablespoons butter
2 tablespoons all-purpose flour
½ cup (3½ oz.) sugar
¼ teaspoon salt
1 cup (8 fl. oz.) milk
2 squares (2 oz.) unsweetened chocolate, grated
½ teaspoon vanilla
½ teaspoon almond extract
4 eggs, separated
½ cup (2 oz.) almonds, roasted and diced

Preheat oven to 400° F. (205° C.).

Melt butter and stir in flour. Add sugar, salt, milk, and chocolate. Cook over medium-low heat, stirring constantly until thickened. Remove sauce from heat; add vanilla and almond extract. In a bowl beat egg whites until stiff; with same beater, beat egg yolks. Stir yolks into chocolate mixture; fold in egg whites and almonds. Turn batter into well-greased 1-quart soufflé dish or casserole. Bake in 400° F. (205° C.) oven for 15 minutes; reduce temperature to 350° F. (180° C.) and continue to bake 20 to 25 minutes. Serve immediately.

16 | WALNUTS
Are You Nutty About Them?

This morning did you wake up with a burning, irresistible desire . . . to become a walnut tree breeder?

You didn't? Well, let's just suppose for a moment that you did anyway, because in a few seconds we are going to find ourselves in a walnut orchard, visiting with a man who will tell us about breeding walnut trees. After talking with him—his name is Dr. Dave Ramos—the odds are walnuts will look just a little bit different the next time we see them in the supermarket.

"Welcome to George Crum's walnut orchard," says Dr. Ramos in greeting. "Say, do you know how to tell you *are* in a walnut orchard?"

We shake our heads "no," so he explains. "Look around you and you'll notice a marked difference on all the trees between the base of the trunk and the smooth bark that begins about two feet off the ground."

You run your fingers over the base of the tree. Here the bark is rough and craggy, while about two feet above the soil line it abruptly becomes smooth and even. The difference is so great, you could probably pick it out speeding past in a car at fifty miles per hour.

"All walnut orchards exhibit that difference between the base and the rest of the trunk. The bottom part is from native American rootstock, while the top is a graft from the English walnut. Although both parts of the graft have 'walnut' in their names, botanically the two are farther apart than an almond and a peach. No other commercial crop shows such a distinct and easily detected difference between the rootstock and the top."

"But why," you ask, "don't people just plant the orchard from walnut seeds?"

"A walnut grower could do this," Ramos answers, "but the resulting trees would be as different from each other as you are different from the people around you."

From a walnut grower's point of view, that much variation would be bad news. Some trees would bear very few nuts, others would have little disease resistance, and all the trees would grow to different sizes and at different rates, thus complicating the harvest. Further, the nuts of some would be tiny, others would have poor keeping qualities, and some would tend to have odd-shaped shells, making it difficult for the processing facilities to crack them.

"The odds of getting a good walnut with none of these undesirable characteristics might be one in thousands," says Ramos.

Owner George Crum joins us. "Here's something else that might interest you!" He reaches up among the leaves of one of his walnut trees and unhooks a lemon-yellow card. "Take a look at it," he invites, as he holds it up towards the sun.

It's about the size of a legal envelope, and as you approach to within about a foot of it, you see some small delta-winged insects on it.

"Those are walnut husk flies," George says, the same sort of enthusiasm in his voice that you'd expect to hear from an elderly senior citizen when referring to a mugger. "But this card is a remarkably efficient trap for keeping them under control and helping us grow our walnuts with fewer chemicals than we used to think we needed."

"How does it work?" you are immediately tempted to ask.

"It contains a perfect imitation of the sex scent that attracts the flies to each other for mating. The scent lures them to the sticky paper on the card and we can get rid of them with nothing more harmful than glue. Before we had these traps, we had to spray every year to control the pest."

George shakes his head philosophically. "A lot of people think we're indifferent to the ecological aspects of artificial chemicals. But you know, even if we didn't care about ecology—which of course we do—we'd still want to do everything we could to minimize the use of chemicals, because they cost so darn much. This pheromone trap—that's its technical name—costs five dollars and can cover at least five acres. If I had to spray every year as a preventive measure, covering the same area would cost $150."

The orchard we're standing in covers about forty acres yet there's hardly a weed to be seen. To anyone who's ever tried to keep a twenty by twenty foot vegetable patch weeded, it's an impressive sight.

"We have to keep it clean during harvest because the way we collect the walnuts is to shake the nuts to the ground and then sweep them into rows, finally gathering them into bins using a special pick-up machine. Come on," he invites, "let's watch how it's done."

A man drives up in something that looks like a large golf cart with a twenty-foot-long hydraulic fist attached. "That's called a shaker machine," Crum explains, pointing toward it. "Rafael Boitez, who's driving it, can shake down all the nuts on a tree at once. We don't want the nuts to drop one by one over a period of weeks, because pests would have time to attack the nuts, and the sun would darken the walnut flesh. Buyers like the light-colored walnuts, and only a few hours in the sun can darken the nutmeats so much that we can lose up to 6 percent of their market value."

As George Crum is speaking, Rafael extends the boom on his machine and it fastens, like a pair of giant tongs, around the trunk of the nearest walnut tree. Rafael pulls a lever and begins shaking the tree, shaking it the way a vibrator belt in a reducing salon might work on your waist. The walnuts cascade to the ground in a twenty-second shower.

We leave our hosts and return home. The odds were right. We never will look at walnuts the same way again. On thinking it over, it would probably be more fun for us to eat walnuts—and they are good for us, supplying potassium, phosphorus, vitamin A, and calcium—rather than breed them. And since we'll be buying them at the market, we'll remember this tip: "Buy them in the shell. They'll last much longer that way and they'll cost less than the shelled ones."

And by the way, if you've never toasted walnuts, you should. Toasting enhances their mellow flavor and eliminates the discoloration that sometimes occurs when they're combined with milk products. It also keeps them good and crispy. To toast, simply spread out your walnuts in a shallow pan and bake in a 350 degree Fahrenheit (180 degree Celsius) oven until golden brown—just about 15 minutes will do it.

Walnuts
in the Menu

COCKTAIL PARTY

Wines   Mixed Drinks

Party Cheese Ball*

Walnut Swiss Cheese Tarts*

Chicken Liver Pâté*

Oven-Barbecued Chicken Wings**

Sliced Cheese Platter

Crackers and Breads

Roasted Soy Walnuts*

*See Walnut Recipes
**See Apricot Recipes

Roasted Soy Walnuts

vegetable oil, as needed
walnuts, shelled, as needed
soy sauce, as needed

Preheat oven to 250° F. (120° C.).
Lightly grease a 9 by 13 inch (23 by 33 cm.) pan. Fill with walnuts. Place pan in oven and bake walnuts for 30 to 45 minutes, or until crisp. Shake pan occasionally to prevent walnuts from sticking. Remove walnuts from oven and sprinkle with soy sauce. Return to oven, stirring occasionally, so nuts get coated with sauce. Remove from oven when sauce has been absorbed.

Party Cheese Ball

½ cup (4 oz.) Roquefort cheese
1 cup (8 oz.) cream cheese
¼ teaspoon garlic salt
1 tablespoon pimiento, chopped
1 tablespoon green pepper, chopped
½ cup (2 oz.) walnuts, toasted
crackers, as needed

Blend Roquefort and cream cheese. Stir in garlic salt, pimiento, and green pepper. Chill until firm. Shape into a ball. Roll ball in toasted walnuts. Chill until serving time. Serve with crackers.

South Seas Walnut Salad

¾ cup (3 oz.) walnuts, coarsely chopped
1½ cups (12 oz.) pineapple chunks
1 cup (6 oz.) celery, chopped
⅓ cup (2⅔ fl. oz.) mayonnaise
1 teaspoon lemon juice
2 tablespoons coconut, flaked
crisp salad greens, as needed

Combine walnuts with pineapple and celery. Mix mayonnaise with lemon juice and coconut, and toss lightly with fruit–walnut mixture. Serve on crisp salad greens.

Chicken Liver Pâté

½ pound chicken livers
2 teaspoons butter
1 tablespoon onion, finely chopped
½ teaspoon curry powder
¼ teaspoon paprika
1 teaspoon seasoned salt
¼ cup (2 fl. oz.) chicken stock
2 cups (16 oz.) cream cheese, softened
1 cup (4 oz.) walnuts, toasted

Sauté chicken livers in butter with onion, curry powder, paprika, and salt until tender. Cool slightly, then turn out contents of the pan into a blender. Add stock and whirl until smooth. Combine cream cheese and chicken liver, mixing until smooth. Cover and chill for several hours to mellow flavors. Stir in walnuts and pile mixture in a serving bowl.

Walnut Salad Athena

Lemon herb dressing:

 ½ cup (4 fl. oz.) olive oil
 ½ cup (4 fl. oz.) lemon juice
 1 tablespoon sugar
 1 teaspoon seasoned salt
 ¼ teaspoon seasoned pepper
 ⅛ teaspoon garlic powder
 ½ teaspoon oregano
 ½ teaspoon marjoram

In a jar, combine olive oil, lemon juice, sugar, salt, pepper, garlic powder, oregano, and marjoram. Cover and shake well until blended.

Salad:

 2 tablespoons butter
 ½ teaspoon dried rosemary, finely crumbled
 1 cup (4 oz.) walnut halves
 12 ounces prawns or large shrimp, cooked and deveined
 1 tablespoon parsley, finely chopped
 2 tablespoons chives or green onion, finely chopped
 crisp salad greens, as needed
 6 radishes, whole or sliced
 6 pitted ripe olives, whole or sliced
 6 pitted stuffed green olives, whole or sliced
 ½ cup (4 oz.) small pickled onions
 3 tomatoes, cut in wedges
 ¾ cup (4½ oz.) Feta or Monterey Jack cheese, cubed

Melt butter with rosemary in heavy skillet. Add walnuts and sauté, stirring now and then, about 5 minutes, over low heat until walnuts are lightly toasted. Remove and cool. Pour dressing over prawns or shrimp. Add parsley and chives or green onion; mix gently, cover, and marinate in refrigerator an hour or longer. When ready to assemble salad, line chilled serving dish with crisp salad greens. Toss radishes, olives, onions, tomatoes, and cheese together with walnuts and prawns until well mixed. Arrange mixture on greens.

Walnut Swiss Cheese Tarts

4 strips bacon
4 green onions, chopped
3 eggs, beaten
1¼ teaspoons salt
¼ teaspoon nutmeg
⅛ teaspoon white pepper
dash cayenne
2 cups (16 fl. oz.) half-and-half
2 cups (12 oz.) Swiss cheese, shredded
1 cup (4 oz.) walnuts, toasted
36 shallow tart shells, unbaked

Preheat oven to 425° F. (220° C.).

Fry bacon until crisp; drain on absorbent paper, then crumble. Measure bacon fat and return 2 tablespoons to skillet. Add onions and sauté until soft but not brown. Combine eggs, salt, nutmeg, white pepper, and cayenne. Mix in half-and-half, cheese, walnuts, bacon, and onions. Spoon mixture into tart shells. Place on baking sheet. Bake for about 15 minutes, just until filling is set and pastry is browned. Serve warm.

Walnut-Spinach Pie with Mushroom Sauce

This crunchy, crustless pie is an easy-to-prepare main dish alternative to meat or poultry.

Pie:

¼ cup (2 fl. oz.) vegetable oil
1 onion, finely chopped
½ cup (3 oz.) celery, finely chopped
¼ cup (1 oz.) parsley, minced
3 cups (12 oz.) walnuts, finely ground
⅛ teaspoon thyme
salt and pepper, to taste
2½ cups (1 lb.) spinach, cooked until just limp and
  chopped
2 eggs, beaten
½ cup (4 oz.) ricotta cheese

Preheat oven to 350° F. (180° C.).

Heat oil in a frying pan and sauté onion, celery, and parsley until soft. Stir in walnuts, thyme, salt, and pepper. Squeeze spinach lightly, place in large bowl, and add nut mixture. Mix eggs and ricotta cheese and add to nut mixture. Shape mixture into a flattened round on a shallow pie plate. Bake for 30 minutes.

Mushroom sauce:

3 tablespoons butter
1⅓ cups (4 oz.) mushrooms, thinly sliced
3 tablespoons all-purpose flour
2 cups (16 fl. oz.) half-and-half
½ teaspoon nutmeg
salt, to taste

Melt butter in a saucepan, add mushrooms, and sauté for 2 or 3 minutes. Remove mushrooms from pan. Add flour to remaining butter and stir. Slowly add half-and-half and stir until thickened. Add nutmeg and salt. To serve, place pie on a platter and pour sauce over it.

Zucchini Walnut Bread

2 eggs, beaten
⅓ cup (2⅔ fl. oz.) vegetable oil
⅓ cup (2⅔ fl. oz.) butter
1 cup (12 fl. oz.) honey or 1½ cups (9½ oz.) brown sugar
1 teaspoon vanilla
2¼ cups (11¼ oz.) unbleached flour
½ cup (2½ oz.) wheat germ
1 tablespoon baking powder
½ teaspoon salt
½ teaspoon cinnamon
2½ cups (15 oz.) zucchini, grated
1 cup (4 oz.) walnuts, chopped

Preheat oven to 325° F. (165° C.).

Combine eggs, oil, butter, honey or brown sugar, and vanilla. Beat well. In another bowl, mix together flour, wheat germ, baking powder, salt, and cinnamon. Mix flour mixture into egg mixture, stirring only enough to combine. Add zucchini and walnuts. Pour batter into two lightly greased 9 by 5 inch (23 by 13 cm.) loaf pans. Bake for 40 minutes, or until knife inserted near center comes out clean.

Chocolate Cookie Sheet Cake

Cake:

  2 cups (10 oz.) all-purpose flour
  2 cups (14 oz.) sugar
  ½ teaspoon salt
  1 cup (8 fl. oz.) butter
  1 cup (8 fl. oz.) water
  3 tablespoons cocoa
  2 eggs, well beaten
  1 teaspoon baking soda
  ½ cup (4 fl. oz.) buttermilk
  1 teaspoon vanilla
  ½ cup (2 oz.) walnuts, finely chopped

Preheat oven to 350° F. (180° C.).

Sift together flour, sugar, and salt. Set aside. In a heavy saucepan, combine butter, water, and cocoa. Bring to a boil and pour over flour mixture. In another bowl, combine eggs, baking soda, buttermilk, and vanilla. Add to flour/butter mixture and mix well. Add walnuts. Pour into a well-greased and floured 10½ by 15½ inch (26.5 by 39 cm.) jelly roll pan. Bake for 20 minutes.

Topping:

  ½ cup (4 fl. oz.) butter
  3 tablespoons cocoa
  6 tablespoons milk
  1 pound powdered sugar
  1 teaspoon vanilla
  1 cup (4 oz.) walnuts, chopped

Begin topping 5 minutes before cake finishes baking. To prepare, in a saucepan combine butter, cocoa, and milk. Bring to a boil over low heat. Remove from heat. Slowly beat in powdered sugar and vanilla. When mixture is smooth, fold in walnuts and spread on warm cake.

Walnut Animal Crackers

2¼ cups (11¼ oz.) all-purpose flour
½ cup (2½ oz.) whole wheat flour
¼ cup (1¼ oz.) yellow cornmeal
1 teaspoon baking powder
¾ teaspoon salt
½ cup (2 oz.) walnuts, finely chopped
⅔ cup (5⅓ fl. oz.) shortening
1 cup (7 oz.) sugar
½ teaspoon vanilla
6 tablespoons milk

Preheat oven to 350° F. (180° C.).

Mix flours with cornmeal, baking powder, salt, and walnuts. Cream shortening with sugar and vanilla. Blend in flour mixture alternately with milk, mixing to a stiff dough. On a lightly floured board, roll small portions at a time to a ⅛-inch (½-cm.) thickness and cut with animal-shaped cookie cutters. Arrange on ungreased cookie sheets. Bake above oven center until edges are lightly browned, about 12 minutes. Cool on wire racks.

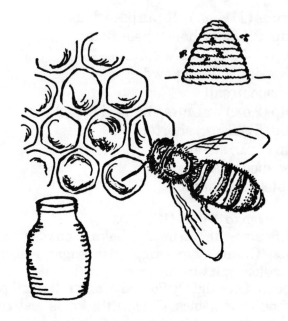

17 | HONEY
How Sweet It Is!

You're dipping a spoon into a jar of golden-amber honey, and already you can almost taste its aromatic sweetness on your breakfast toast.

But wait! There's a story behind that honey. To produce the honey in that one-pound jar, bees had to fly a distance equivalent to three times around the world at the equator. If your honey was made on an average summer day, more than fifty thousand bees worked from dawn to dusk to gather the necessary nectar.

And while they were doing that, they were also doing something of incomparable value to man. Did you know that a third of all the crops we eat need honey bees for pollination? Without honey bees, we'd have no almonds,

no prunes, no melons, no apples, no carrots, no onions...
the list goes on and on.

Our grazing animals would be in trouble too, for without bees, there would be no alfalfa or clover. Wildlife also depends on thousands of varieties of fruits, nuts, and seeds that need honey bees for pollination.

"In fact," declares Professor Norman Gary, of the University of California at Davis, "bees are as important to many of our crops as fertilizer, water, or even sunlight."

The beeswax they produce is useful to us, too. Candles, lipstick, crayons, and shoe polish may have beeswax among their ingredients.

Although three hundred thousand Americans keep bees as a hobby, there are only three thousand full-time beekeepers in the United States. Beekeeping is an arduous life. To maintain a family of four, a beekeeper needs the income from close to one thousand hives—which means a minimum of 50 million bees.

"Bees require care, just like any other farm animal," points out Dr. Gary. "You have to protect them from diseases, you worry when it gets too hot or cold, and you have to move the hives to good foraging areas just as surely as a shepherd has to move his sheep to good grazing lands."

The beekeeper's worst worry is pesticides. Supposedly County Extension offices warn nearby beekeepers whenever a farmer is going to use a pesticide, but the process doesn't always work. And even if a beekeeper is notified, if his thousand or more hives are scattered in three counties, he has to fly around like Superman to rescue his tiny charges from the danger of sprays.

It is not necessarily honey that keeps a beekeeper in business. In rich agricultural areas, such as California's Sacramento Valley, a beekeeper can make more money from renting his bees to farmers. The going rate for pollinating an almond crop in 1981 averaged $22 per hive during the blooming season. When that season finishes, the beekeeper can rent his hives for up to three times more to pollinate such successive crops as prunes, melons, or alfalfa.

Honey is a natural sweet. It's composed of fructose, which gives it flavor, and glucose, which together with the fructose provides quick energy. And in all its forms—liquid, creamed, or combed—it has no sodium and no additives.

Need some tips on how to store and use your honey? Jerry Marston, a bee expert at the University of California at Davis, notes that one thing we don't have to worry about is shelf life. "Honey stored in the tombs in ancient Egypt is still edible," he reveals.

Howard Foster, a beekeeper and past president of the American Beekeeping Federation, adds, "It will keep practically forever, but in time, most honeys will crystallize. To make it liquid again, all you do is heat the container in hot—not boiling—water until the contents become clear."

Honey can be substituted for granulated sugar in a recipe that calls for no more than a cup of sweetening. In making the switch, use two-thirds cup of honey for the one cup of sugar and, if baking, reduce oven temperature by 25 degrees Fahrenheit (15 degrees Celsius).

How do beekeepers like to use their product? If you should ever visit the Bee Biology Laboratory at Davis and Dr. Gary invites you to come in for a cup of coffee, don't expect him to offer you white sugar to go along with your brew. Dr. Gary and his colleagues would find that a bore. Instead, they offer a variety of honeys.

"The flavors of honeys," explains Dr. Gary, "are as different from each other as different flavors of ice cream. Ice cream, however, offers only a narrow choice, maybe thirty or forty flavors. But honey! You have thousands of varieties . . . as many different taste sensations as there are kinds of flowers that produce nectar." So why not buy a selection of honeys and experiment with different flavors in your coffee or tea?

❧ ❧

Honey
in the Menu

DINNER

Ice Cold Beer or California Chenin Blanc

Golden Glow Chicken (with rice omitted)*

Delaware Crackling Bread*

Grandma's Pickled Apricots**

Sweet and Sour Spinach Salad*

Honey Chocolate Freezer Cake*

Coffee or Tea

*See Honey Recipes
**See Apricot Recipes

❧ ❧

Cheese-Filled Coffee Cake

Dough:

> 1 package dry yeast
> ¼ cup (2 fl oz.) water, lukewarm
> 1 teaspoon honey
> 1 egg, lightly beaten
> ¾ cup (6 fl oz.) butter
> 2 cups (10 oz.) all-purpose flour
> ¼ teaspoon salt

Preheat oven to 375° F. (190° C.).

To prepare dough, mix yeast, water, and honey. Let stand for 10 minutes. Add egg. Cut butter into flour and salt and mix well. Add yeast mixture and blend completely. Divide into two balls and roll each into 8 by 10 inch (20 by 25 cm.) rectangles.

Filling:

> 2 cups (16 oz.) cream cheese
> ½ cup (6 fl oz.) honey
> ½ teaspoon vanilla
> 1 teaspoon lemon juice.

To prepare filling, combine cream cheese, honey, vanilla, and lemon juice. Spread half the filling on each rectangle and fold horizontally in thirds by taking each long side toward the middle, making one side overlap the other a little where the two meet. Fold each end up about 1½ inches (4 cm.)

Bake immediately for 25 minutes. Serve warm.

Delaware Crackling Bread

6 slices thick-sliced bacon, diced
2 tablespoons onion, chopped
1½ cups (7½ oz.) yellow corn meal
½ cup (2½ oz.) all-purpose flour
3 teaspoons baking powder
½ teaspoon baking soda
1½ teaspoons salt
2 eggs
2 tablespoons honey
½ cup (4 fl oz.) buttermilk
1 cup (8 fl oz.) fresh orange juice

Preheat oven to 350° F. (180° C.).

In a 9-inch (23-cm.) oven-proof skillet, cook bacon until crisp. Add onions and cook until tender (but not brown). Remove bacon and onions and drain off all but 2 table-spoons fat. In a large bowl, mix together corn meal, flour, baking powder, baking soda, and salt. Beat together eggs, honey, buttermilk, and orange juice. Add liquid mixture to dry ingredients all at once. Stir until just blended. Stir in bacon and onions. Spoon batter into hot skillet and bake for 30 to 35 minutes. Serve hot from the skillet with butter and honey.

Sweet-and-Sour Spinach Salad

2 large bunches fresh spinach, washed and dried
8 slices bacon
½ cup (4 fl oz.) tarragon vinegar, or more to taste
¾ cup (9 fl oz.) honey
4 teaspoons lemon peel, grated
juice of 1 lemon
2 eggs, hard-cooked and grated
¼ cup (1½ oz.) Cheddar cheese, grated

Remove stems from spinach and place leaves on a serving plate. Chill while preparing dressing. Fry bacon until very crisp. Drain and reserve fat. To bacon drippings, add vinegar and honey. Simmer for 2 minutes. Add crumbled bacon, lemon peel, and lemon juice. Spoon hot dressing over chilled spinach. Garnish with grated egg and cheese. Serve immediately.

Stir-Fry Zucchini and Carrots

2 tablespoons butter
2 tablespoons vegetable oil
6 medium zucchinis, cut into strips
6 medium carrots, cut into strips
2 tablespoons honey
1 tablespoon lemon juice
salt and freshly ground pepper, to taste

Heat butter and oil in a large skillet or wok over high heat. Add zucchinis and carrots and stir-fry until crisp-tender. Add honey and lemon juice, tossing lightly. Season to taste with salt and pepper. Serve immediately.

Beef Stew, Flemish Style

2 pounds boneless beef chuck or round
3 medium onions
¼ cup (2 fl oz.) butter
¼ cup (1¼ oz.) all-purpose flour
1½ teaspoons salt
¼ teaspoon pepper
2 cloves garlic, minced
1 bay leaf
½ teaspoon thyme
1 tablespoon cider vinegar
1 tablespoon honey
1 bottle (12 fl oz.) beer, dark type
3 cups (8 oz.) noodles, cooked and hot

Preheat oven to 325° F. (165° C.).

Cut meat into 1-inch (2½-cm.) cubes. Slice onions as thinly as possible. Melt half the butter in a large, heavy skillet. Sauté onions until limp and golden brown. Transfer onions to a casserole with a tight-fitting lid. Combine flour, salt, and pepper in a bag. Add meat and shake to coat. Add remaining butter to skillet and brown meat on all sides. Add to onions in casserole. To beef mixture, add garlic, bay leaf, thyme, vinegar, honey, and beer, and stir to blend. Cover and bake in oven for 2 hours, or until meat is fork-tender. Serve over noodles.

Golden-Glow Chicken

2 tablespoons butter
2 tablespoons vegetable oil
8 pieces chicken
2 tablespoons onion, chopped
2 cloves garlic, minced
½ teaspoon chili powder
½ teaspoon cumin
¾ cup (6 fl oz.) orange juice
1 teaspoon orange peel, grated
1 tablespoon honey
3 to 4 cups (8 oz. to 12 oz.) rice, cooked and hot
1 tablespoon cornstarch
1 cup (8 fl oz.) yogurt or sour cream
salt and pepper, to taste
1 orange, peeled and sliced
2 tablespoons parsley, chopped

In a large skillet, heat butter and oil, add chicken, and brown on all sides. Add onion, garlic, chili powder, cumin, orange juice, orange peel, and honey. Cover and simmer until chicken is tender, about 15 minutes, turning pieces once. Place chicken on rice. Mix cornstarch into yogurt or sour cream, stir into pan juices, and cook until just thickened. Add salt and pepper. Pour sauce over chicken and garnish with orange slices and parsley.

Lemon-Honey Squares

1 cup (7 oz.) sugar
2¼ cups (11¼ oz.) all-purpose flour
¼ teaspoon salt
1 cup (8 fl oz.) butter

1 cup (4 oz.) coconut, flaked
1 cup (12 fl oz.) honey
2 tablespoons butter
¼ cup (2 fl oz.) lemon juice
1 teaspoon lemon peel, grated
3 eggs, beaten

Preheat oven to 350° F. (180° C.).

In a mixing bowl, combine sugar, flour, salt, butter, and coconut. Mix well. Put two-thirds of the mixture in an ungreased 9-inch (23-cm.) square pan. Set aside.

In a small saucepan, combine honey, butter, lemon juice, lemon peel, and eggs. Cook over medium heat, stirring constantly, until mixture thickens. Remove from heat and allow to cool. Spread honey mixture over dough in pan. Crumble remaining dough on top. Bake for 30 minutes. Cut into small squares and cool in a pan on a rack.

California Nut Pie

3 eggs, well beaten
1⅓ cups (16 fl oz.) honey
⅛ teaspoon salt
1 teaspoon vanilla
½ cup (4 fl oz.) butter, melted
1¼ cups (5 oz.) walnuts, almonds, or pecans,
    chopped
1 9-inch (23-cm.) pie shell, unbaked
vanilla ice cream (optional)

Preheat oven to 350° F. (180° C.).

Combine eggs with honey, salt, vanilla, and butter. Stir in nuts. Pour into pie shell. Bake for 40 to 45 minutes. Top with vanilla ice cream, if used.

Honey-Chocolate Freezer Cake

⅔ cup (5⅓ fl oz.) butter, softened
1¼ cups (15 fl oz.) honey
⅓ cup (1½ oz.) cocoa
2 eggs
1 teaspoon vanilla
2½ cups (12½ oz.) all-purpose flour
1½ teaspoons baking soda
½ teaspoon salt
1 cup (8 fl. oz.) milk
1 quart vanilla ice cream

Preheat oven to 325° F. (165° C.).

Cream butter and gradually add honey and cocoa. Mix well. Beat in the eggs one at a time. Add vanilla.

Sift together the flour, baking soda, and salt. Add to the butter mixture, alternately with milk, beating constantly. Pour batter into two 8-inch (20-cm.) cake pans and bake for 35 minutes, or until a toothpick comes out clean. Cool.

Fill cake with vanilla ice cream and frost with honey-flavored whipped cream (recipe follows). Chill in freezer.

Whipped Cream with Honey

2 cups (16 fl oz.) heavy cream
4 tablespoons honey
2 teaspoons vanilla
dash salt

Chill beaters, bowl, and cream. Whip cream until soft peaks form, then slowly beat in honey, vanilla, and salt. Beat until well combined.

SECTION
4

DAIRY FOODS

18 | EGGS
Incredible and Edible

If there's anyone in the world who knows a lot about eggs, it's Jim Williams, Vice President for Operations of Nu-laid Foods, Incorporated. If the 900 million-plus eggs handled each year by this co-op were placed end to end, they'd reach from the processing plant in Ripon, California, to New York City and back—*eighteen times.*

Williams' comprehensive knowledge of eggs is particularly evident when he's talking about eggs and nutrition. "Did you know," says Williams, "that eggs are second only to mother's milk in protein value? In fact, an egg is so near perfection that scientists use it as a standard to measure the value of protein in all other foods."

According to Williams, if you have a scale ranking

quality—not quantity—of protein measuring from 1 to 100, mother's milk would fit right at the top, with a rating of 95 to 100. Eggs would be a very close second at 94. Cow's milk would be third at 85 to 90, while meat and fish would be fourth at 76 to 85. Rice would rank fifth at 60 to 70, while lower ratings would be given to potatoes, soybeans, grains, and so on.

What about eggs and cholesterol? Williams has a strong opinion on that. "The normal human body manufactures up to 2000 milligrams of cholesterol a day while an egg contains only 275 milligrams."

Williams loves to tell stories about the egg business. "Several years ago," he begins, a certain glee detectable in his voice, "the manufacturers of egg noodles were in b-i-g trouble." The problem was that the USDA had banned the artificial food colorings the noodle manufacturers used for their golden egg noodles.

"Who would buy pasty-white 'golden' egg noodles?" wonders Williams. "But," he goes on, "we egg people had a solution for them. You see, the color of an egg yolk is controlled by what you feed the hen. If you feed the hen more corn and alfalfa than usual, you'll get a darker yolk. We measure yolk color by a scale of 1 to 5, called the NEPA scale. The egg yolks we're used to are somewhere between 1 and 2 on the NEPA scale. The top end of the scale is a brilliant sunset-orange that would look very strange to the average consumer."

And what does all this have to do with the noodle manufacturers' dilemma? "We just asked members of our cooperative to supply eggs from hens which had eaten lots and lots of corn and alfalfa. In no time we were getting yolks with a NEPA rating of 5 . . . but we found we'd overshot . . . the macaroni was too bright."

By fine-tuning the diet of the chickens, the growers discovered that a 4.5 NEPA rating could exactly compensate for the missing artificial food coloring. "The macaroni and noodle manufacturers now make their product with as much eye-appeal as ever, and they don't need to use one trace of artificial food coloring."

Warren Johnson is another man in the egg business, but he's closer to the farm end of it. He looks after close to sixty thousand laying hens in his football-field-size poultry houses. Johnson has a tip for people who bake with his product. "If you're going to beat your egg whites and you want the highest possible volume, leave the whole egg in its shell at room temperature for a day, or better . . . two days."

When asked if they might go bad in two days, Johnson shakes his head in an emphatic *no*. "Professional bakers do it all the time. An egg inside its shell is completely sterile."

Nancy Bolduc, from the California Egg Advisory Board, recommends that eggs be refrigerated in just about all other circumstances, though. "Keep them in the carton with the large end of the eggs up and they'll last at least a month. In fact, if you store them this way for a few days before hard-boiling, they'll be easier to peel. That's because a little bit of air is taken in through the pores of the egg and forms an isolating layer between the shell membranes."

Warren Johnson has an additional tip for shoppers who come home with a dozen eggs and find that one or two have cracks. "Don't throw the egg away unless the inner membrane is leaking. Your egg is still sterile inside . . . but it's probably a good idea to cook the egg rather than using it raw for something like eggnog."

Cooking with eggs is quick and easy. Just be sure to use moderate temperatures—heat that's too high will turn the whites tough and rubbery and the yolks greenish. That green is from iron and sulfur compounds that form when the egg is overcooked. While it won't hurt you, it's just not an egg at its beautiful best.

Eggs
in the Menu

WINTER BRUNCH

Gold-Strike Punch*   Old-Fashioneds

Sunny Winter Omelets*

Chris' Cloud Sandwiches*

Peachy Ham Slices**

Fresh Winter Fruits

Coffee or Tea

*See Egg Recipes
**See Peach Recipes

Gold-Strike Punch

6 eggs, slightly beaten
6 cups (48 fl. oz.) orange juice, chilled
⅓ cup (4 fl. oz.) honey
orange or lemon sherbet, as needed

Combine eggs, orange juice, and honey. Beat well until thoroughly blended. Pour into a punch bowl. Add sherbet in scoops.
Makes 15 punch cup servings, or 8 mugfuls.

Eggaroni

2 tablespoons butter
2 tablespoons all-purpose flour
2 cups (16 fl. oz.) milk
9 eggs, hard cooked
3 eggs, beaten
2 cups (3½ oz.) elbow macaroni, cooked
½ cup (3 oz.) celery, chopped
¼ cup (1½ oz.) onion, chopped
1 teaspoon seasoned salt
¾ teaspoon marjoram
⅛ teaspoon pepper

Preheat oven to 350° F. (180° C.).
Melt butter in a large saucepan. Blend in flour and cook, stirring until mixture is smooth and bubbly. Stir in milk all at once. Heat to boiling, stirring constantly. Reserve 4 center egg slices from the hard-cooked eggs for garnish; chop remaining hard-cooked eggs. Stir chopped eggs, beaten eggs, macaroni, celery, onion, seasoned salt, marjoram, and pepper into milk mixture. Pour into a

greased 1½-quart (48-oz.) casserole. Bake for 35 to 40 minues, or until casserole is heated thoroughly. Garnish with reserved egg slices. Serve hot.

World's Easiest Soufflé

This soufflé is slightly richer and heavier than the traditional version but can be readied for the oven in only 5 minutes.

butter, as needed
grated Parmesan cheese, as needed
4 eggs
⅔ cup (4 oz.) sharp Cheddar cheese, coarsely grated
⅓ cup (3 oz.) cream cheese
⅓ cup (2⅔ fl. oz.) milk or half-and-half
¼ cup (1 oz.) Parmesan cheese, grated
½ teaspoon onion salt
½ teaspoon dry mustard

Preheat oven to 350° F. (180° C.).

Butter bottom and sides of 1-quart (32-oz.) soufflé dish or casserole. Dust with Parmesan cheese. Set aside. In a blender container, combine eggs, cheddar cheese, cream cheese, milk or half-and-half, ¼ cup Parmesan cheese, onion salt, and mustard. Cover and blend at medium speed until smooth, about 30 seconds. Blend at high speed another 10 to 15 seconds. Carefully pour into prepared dish. Bake for 25 to 30 minutes, or until puffy and delicately browned. Serve immediately.

Chris' Cloud Sandwiches

4 slices day-old bread
butter, as needed
2 slices Swiss or Cheddar cheese
2 slices cooked ham
4 eggs
1 cup (8 fl. oz.) milk
½ teaspoon dry mustard
dash pepper

Preheat oven to 350° F. (180° C.).

Trim crust from bread. Butter bread on one side. Place two slices of bread, buttered side down, in a 9 by 5 inch (23 by 13 cm.) loaf pan. Top each with cheese, ham, and the remaining bread, buttered side up. Beat together eggs, milk, mustard, and pepper. Pour over sandwiches. Bake for 40 to 45 minutes, or until knife inserted near center comes out clean.

Sunny Winter Omelet

½ banana, peeled and sliced
¼ cup (1 oz.) flaked coconut
4 eggs
¼ cup (2 fl. oz.) water
½ teaspoon salt
dash pepper
1 tablespoon butter

Combine banana and coconut. Set aside. Mix eggs, water, salt, and pepper with a fork. Heat butter in a 10-inch (25-cm.) omelet pan or skillet until just hot enough to sizzle a drop of water. Pour in egg mixture. It should set at edges at once. With a metal spatula, carefully draw cooked edges to center. Slide pan back and forth to keep mixture in motion and sliding freely. While top is still creamy, spread ¼ cup of the banana mixture on half the omelet. Fold omelet in half or roll, turning it out onto a platter. Top with remaining filling.

Oriental Omelet

½ cup (4 oz.) chicken, cooked and chopped
¼ cup (1½ oz.) bean sprouts
3 water chestnuts, sliced
1 teaspoon soy sauce
4 eggs
¼ cup (2 fl. oz.) water
2 tablespoons green pepper, chopped
½ teaspoon onion, minced
½ teaspoon salt
dash pepper
1 tablespoon butter

Combine chicken, bean sprouts, water chestnuts, and soy sauce. Set aside.

Mix eggs, water, green pepper, onion, salt, and pepper with a fork. Heat butter in a 10-inch (25-cm.) omelet pan or skillet until just hot enough to sizzle a drop of water. Pour in egg mixture. With a pancake turner, carefully draw cooked portions at edges toward center. Slide pan rapidly back and forth over heat to keep mixture in motion. While top is still creamy, arrange chicken mixture on half the omelet. Fold omelet in half or roll, turning it out onto platter.

Puffy Strawberry Omelet

¼ cup (2 fl. oz.) sour cream
1¼ cups (9 oz.) strawberries, hulled and sliced
½ teaspoon grated orange peel
4 eggs, separated
¼ cup (2 fl. oz.) water
¼ teaspoon salt
¼ teaspoon cream of tartar
1 tablespoon butter

Preheat oven to 350° F. (180° C.).

Measure out sour cream, strawberries, and orange peel. Set aside. Beat egg yolks until thick and lemon colored, about 5 minutes. Add water, salt, and cream of tartar to whites. Beat whites until stiff but not dry. Fold yolks into whites. Heat butter in a 10-inch (25-cm.) omelet pan or skillet with an oven-proof handle. Pour in egg mixture and gently level the surface. Reduce heat to medium and cook for 5 minutes, or until lightly browned on bottom. Bake for 10 to 12 minutes, or until knife inserted halfway between center and outside edge comes out clean. Loosen edges with a spatula. Down the center of the omelet, cut through surface with a sharp knife. Spread 2 tablespoons sour cream on one half; sprinkle with ½ cup strawberries. Fold omelet in half and turn out onto platter. Spread remaining sour cream over omelet and top with remaining strawberries and orange peel. Serve immediately.

Pots de Crème

1 cup (6 oz.) semi-sweet chocolate bits
½ cup (4 fl. oz.) strong coffee, hot
4 eggs
3 tablespoons sugar
1 teaspoon brandy or rum extract
1 cup (8 fl. oz.) heavy cream

Place chocolate pieces in blender container. Blend at medium speed for 10 seconds. Scrape down sides of blender container with a rubber spatula, if necessary. Add coffee. Blend at medium speed for 5 seconds. Add eggs, sugar, brandy or rum extract. Blend at medium speed until smooth, about 30 to 45 seconds. Pour into 6 pot de crème cups, tiny bowls, or sherbet glasses. Refrigerate overnight.

To serve, whip cream and use as a garnish.

19 | MILK
It Doesn't Grow in Cartons

"In thirty-two years, we've almost never had a vacation."

Surprisingly, Cecelia Mello isn't complaining at all, she's just explaining what it's like to have a dairy herd. The fact is, she loves her life as part of a dairy family, but she happens to know from her own experience that dairy farming can be an almost unbelievably restrictive way of life.

"We have to get up at 4:00 A.M. to milk the cows. The cleaning, feeding, milking again, and other work won't end until 7:00 P.M. And that's on good days. Sometimes, if a calf is sick or a cow is calving, we may have to stay up around the clock."

It's easy to imagine Cecelia Mello staying up with a sick calf. She looks like everyone's image of a perfect grandmother—warm, maternal, nice to be near. One senses that she really cares about her animals, that she feels an affection for them.

But no matter how much she cares, there's still the fact that taking care of them is a lot of work. "Cows must be fed and milked twice a day, seven days a week," Mello points out. "They don't stop needing to be milked just because it's a weekend or a holiday or your son's graduation."

Running a dairy farm is a lot more than just milking cows. Cecelia Mello finds that between herself and her husband, they must be bookkeepers, veterinarians, mechanics, electricians, lawyers, financial managers, and agronomists, as well as farm hands.

"If we didn't develop these skills," says Mello, "we'd have to hire expensive outside help, and in a short time there would be a 'for sale' sign hanging out on our barn."

Twenty-five years ago there were over 2 million dairy farmers in the United States, but their number has dwindled today to less than half a million. The long hours Mello speaks of, together with no vacations, uncertain income, hard work, government regulations, and the expansion of cities onto farmland, all have taken their toll.

But for those like Mello, who choose to stay, it's a life they love. Jill Martin loves this kind of life and adds, "It's a wonderful environment for raising kids." Others explain that they enjoy being their own boss, they like working with animals, and many, many say they like knowing they provide an important service.

Dairy farmers have a tremendous commitment to their product. George Gambonini proudly points out that two eight-ounce glasses of milk will provide about a third of an adult's protein requirements. "The same two glasses," he goes on to say, "will also meet 72 percent of an adult's daily calcium needs. You get all this nutrition and more for only about 11 percent of your calorie allowance if you're an average man or 14 percent if you're a woman."

The calcium Gambonini refers to is important not only for strong teeth and bones, but also for normal nerve function, rhythmical heart beat, muscle control, and normal blood coagulation. Yet according to Dr. Robert Marcus, a Stanford University Medical School researcher, some studies show that the average American consumes less than half the recommended amount of calcium each day.

Dr. Roslyn Alfin-Slater, a nutrition professor at the University of California, Los Angeles, adds, "While calcium is found in other foods, they are not practical sources of this important mineral in the traditional United States diet. This is why the USDA in their Daily Food Guide recommends that adults consume two or more glasses of milk or its calcium equivalent from the milk group each day."

If you want to substitute other milk products for whole milk, the California Milk Advisory Board suggests these calcium equivalents: a half cup of cottage cheese or yogurt equals the same amount of milk; a half cup of ice cream equals one-third of a cup of milk.

Did you know that milk and cereal together are better for you than either one alone? That's because lysine and tryptophan, two essential amino acids, are abundant in milk, while cereals are deficient in them. Eaten together, a complete protein is formed—and that's good for you.

Back in our recent past, the milkman usually brought just one kind of milk to the door—whole and unhomogenized, with a thick creamy layer of "top milk" just right for pouring over cereal. Today, you'll find at least five fluid milk types available containing different amounts of milk fat. They range from "nonfat," which is not more than .25 percent milk fat, to "extra-rich," which is about 3.5 percent milk fat. Similarly, dried forms of milk range from nonfat to whole milk, and canned milk can be evaporated (concentrated by the removal of about half of its water) or sweetened condensed (where part of the water has been removed and sugar added).

Heat and light destroy milk's nutrients, so keep it refrigerated in a closed container.

Jill Martin recommends that you give a nutrition-packed milk drink to your family for breakfast or a snack. "They don't even know how good it is for them," Jill confides, "they just know that it tastes good."

Milk
in the Menu

LUNCH

California Colombard

Spinach Cheese Soufflé*

Green Salad

Crusty Rolls and Butter

Lemon Milk Sherbet*

Georgia Apple Bars**

Coffee or Tea

*See Milk Recipes
**See Apple Recipes

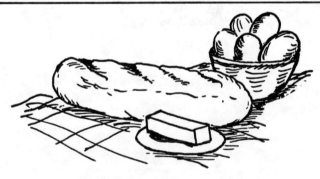

Breakfast Flip

Here's a nutritious and speedy breakfast that one dairy farmer's wife uses as a way to get her family to eat an egg without tasting it.

    1 egg
    1 cup (8 fl. oz.) milk
    1 cup (8 fl. oz.) fresh orange juice
    5 ice cubes

Place all ingredients in a blender and blend on high speed until ice is completely crushed. Serve in a tall glass with a straw.

Cream of Fresh Pea Soup

    3 tablespoons butter
    ⅔ cup (4 oz.) celery, chopped
    ⅓ cup (2 oz.) green onion, chopped
    1 pound peas, shelled
    4 cups (1 qt.) milk
    1 teaspoon salt
    ½ teaspoon sugar
    ¾ teaspoon basil, crumbled
    ⅛ teaspoon nutmeg
    ⅛ teaspoon pepper
    2 tablespoons almonds, sliced (optional)

Melt butter in a saucepan. Sauté celery and onion until limp. Add peas, milk, salt, sugar, basil, nutmeg, and pepper. Bring to a boil. Cover and simmer for 25 minutes or until peas are very tender. Whir mixture in electric blender to puree. Reheat, stirring, until hot. Serve with a sprinkling of sliced almonds on top, if used.

Clam Chowder

1 cup (6 oz.) zucchini, sliced ⅜-inch (1-cm.) thick
½ cup (3 oz). carrots, thinly sliced
½ cup (3 oz.) onion, chopped
⅛ teaspoon garlic, minced
1 tablespoon butter
1¼ cups (10 oz.) whole baby clams, with liquid
¼ teaspoon thyme, crumbled
⅛ teaspoon pepper
1 cup (8 fl. oz.) milk

Combine zucchini, carrots, onion, garlic, and butter. Cover and cook for 5 minutes, stirring occasionally. Add liquid from clams, thyme, and pepper. Cover and simmer 5 minutes longer, or until vegetables are tender-crisp. Add clams and milk. Heat thoroughly.

Spinach Cheese Soufflé

½ pound spinach
1 tablespoon butter
3 tablespoons all-purpose flour
1 cup (8 fl. oz.) milk
5 eggs, separated
½ teaspoon salt
several grinds black pepper
¾ cup (3 oz.) Parmesan cheese, grated

Preheat oven to 375° F. (190° C.).
Wash and trim spinach. Place in saucepan. Add 1 inch of water, cover, and cook over medium heat until limp. Drain, squeeze dry, and chop finely. In a saucepan, melt butter and blend in flour. Stir in milk. Cook, stirring,

until sauce thickens and boils. Remove from heat and stir in egg yolks. Stir in spinach, salt, pepper, and cheese. Cool to lukewarm. Whip egg whites until stiff. Fold into spinach mixture. Turn into 5-cup (40-oz.) soufflé dish. Bake for 30 minutes, or until puffed and light golden brown. Serve at once.

Quick and Easy Fish Curry

¼ cup (2 fl. oz.) butter
2 onions, cut into wedges
1 large clove garlic, minced
1 teaspoon curry powder
¼ cup (1½ oz.) all-purpose flour
2 cups (16 fl. oz.) milk
1 teaspoon salt
1 pound fish fillets, cut into bite-size pieces
2 to 3 cups (6 to 8 oz.) cooked rice, hot
1 tomato, cut in chunks
4 slices bacon, cooked and crumbled
2 tablespoons green onion, sliced

Melt butter in skillet. Add onions and garlic and sauté briefly until tender. Stir in curry powder and cook ½ minute. Blend in flour. Remove from heat. In another skillet, heat milk and salt to boiling, stirring now and then. Add fish and return to boil. Simmer 5 minutes. Spoon some hot milk into onion mixture and stir to blend. Add remaining milk and fish to onion mixture and cook, stirring, until it is thickened and comes to boil. Serve over rice. Garnish with tomato, bacon, and green onion.

Roast Beef and Gravy Dinner

1 beef roast
potatoes, as needed
all-purpose flour, as needed
beef stock, as needed
milk, as needed
salt and pepper, to taste

Preheat oven to 550° F. (290° C.).

Place beef fat side up in a shallow roasting pan. Scrub potatoes, cut a small slice from one end of each, and place around beef. Insert a meat thermometer into the thickest part of the roast and place pan in 550° F. (290° C.) oven. Immediately reduce heat to 350° F. (180° C.) and roast until thermometer reaches 135° F. (57° C.) to 145° F. (63° C.) (for medium rare), about 18 to 20 minutes per pound. Remove roast from oven, and place on a serving platter. Place pan with drippings on a hot burner. Estimate amount of drippings, and blend in an equal amount of flour. Stir well with a wide, flat-bottomed wooden spoon. Slowly add enough beef stock to form the consistency of a thick cream sauce. Add milk to equal beef stock and simmer for 10 to 15 minutes. Add salt and pepper. Thin with milk, if necessary.

To serve, pour gravy over beef and potatoes.

Café Au Lait Dessert

½ cup (3½ oz.) sugar
2 tablespoons instant coffee
1 envelope plain gelatin
1 teaspoon orange peel, grated
¼ teaspoon cinnamon
⅛ teaspoon salt
3 cups (24 fl. oz.) milk
3 eggs, separated
1 teaspoon vanilla extract
orange peel curls (optional)

In the top of a double boiler, combine sugar, coffee, gelatin, orange peel, cinnamon, salt, and milk. Stir in egg yolks. Cook over boiling water, stirring, until mixture thickens slightly, about 6 to 8 minutes. Refrigerate custard until it begins to stiffen. Remove from refrigerator and stir in vanilla. Whip egg whites until stiff. Fold into custard mixture. Pour into 4-cup (32-oz.) soufflé dish.* Chill until firm. Carefully remove foil. Garnish with orange peel curls, if used.

*Prepare soufflé dish by tying heavy foil around the outside, with the top of the paper extending 2 to 3 inches above the dish.

Graham Cracker Cream Pie

1 cup (6 oz.) graham cracker crumbs
½ cup (3½ oz.) sugar
½ cup (4 fl. oz.) butter, melted
3 tablespoons cornstarch
2 cups (16 fl. oz.) milk
3 eggs, separated
½ cup (3½ oz.) sugar
1 teaspoon vanilla
1 tablespoon sugar
½ teaspoon baking powder

Preheat oven to 325° F. (165° C.).

Stir together graham cracker crumbs, ½ cup (3½ oz.) sugar, and butter. Press mixture into a 9-inch (23-cm.) pie pan, reserving ⅓ cup (2 oz.). Set aside.

In a small bowl, combine cornstarch and ½ cup (4 fl. oz.) milk. Stir until very smooth. In a double boiler, combine egg yolks, remaining milk, ½ cup (3½ oz.) sugar, and vanilla. Stir well. Slowly add cornstarch mixture and cook until mixture thickens.

In a large bowl, beat egg whites until thick. Add 1 tablespoon sugar and the baking powder and beat until mixture forms a thick meringue.

Pour filling into pie shell and top with meringue. Sprinkle reserved crumbs on top. Bake for 20 minutes, or until meringue is lightly browned. Cool, chill, and keep refrigerated. Serve well chilled.

Lemon-Milk Sherbet

3 to 4 lemons
1 envelope plain gelatin
3 cups (24 fl. oz.) milk
dash salt
1 cup (7 oz.) sugar
2 egg whites

Grate 1 firmly packed tablespoon of peel from lemon. Halve and squeeze lemons to get ¾ cup (6 fl. oz.) juice. Combine gelatin, 1 cup (8 fl. oz.) milk, and salt in saucepan. Stir over medium heat until gelatin dissolves. Stir in sugar. Heat, stirring, until sugar dissolves. Add remaining milk, lemon peel, and lemon juice. Turn mixture out into glass 9 by 5-inch (23 by 13-cm.) loaf pan or plastic refrigerator container. Freeze, stirring now and then, until mixture is softly frozen throughout. Turn into mixer bowl with egg whites. Whip until fluffy. Return to pan or container. Freeze until firm.

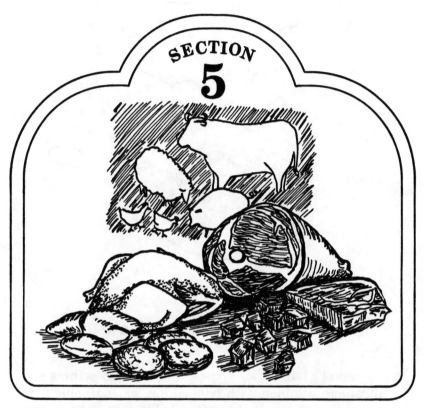

MEAT AND POULTRY

20 | BEEF
You Have a Steak in It

The camel's hair in an artist's brush has something significant in common with bone china, photographic film, and leather shoes, but you'd probably have a hard time guessing just what . . . unless you happen to be part of the beef industry.

All these items come from beef. The "camel's hair" in artists' brushes really comes from the little hairs in beef cattle's ears. Bone china is made, in part, from beef bones. Leather shoes are usually made from beef hides, and the gelatin in both marshmallows and photographic film comes from beef bones and hooves. The fact is, there's a lot more to the story of beef than the steak you buy in the supermarket.

The beef industry is also a lot different now from the image we used to have of it from John Wayne movies. David Shiffman, mayor of Santa Barbara, California, and member of a cattle-ranching family, tells, as an example, how his young son used to ruin every piece of lawn furniture practicing with his lariat. The child thought being a cowboy was really "where it was at." But Shiffman had to say, "Look here, son, all this is changing. When you grow up, you'll have to turn in your lariat for a hand-held calculator. You'll have to get off old Buck and learn to fly a helicopter instead. And it's not lonely nights home on the range; it will be delicate management-labor negotiations."

That's if the family stays in business. The beef industry is precariously cyclical. Unlike other industries, beef production can't react quickly to supply and demand factors; about two to two-and-a-half years go by from the time a calf is conceived until it is ready for market. Meanwhile, the costs for feed, transportation, energy, and other factors can increase so fast that in some years ranchers lose money on every animal sold.

While each year some ranchers are forced to sell their land, or else put it to alternate uses, those who still cling to cattle ranching as a way of life do so, as Sue Shannon says, "because it's a heritage we're proud of. We'll try to preserve it no matter what!"

If you want to be a smart shopper for beef, the manager of the California Beef Council, Constance Bennet, suggests, "Figure cost per edible serving rather than cost per pound. Some boneless cuts, although priced higher than bone-in cuts, may be better buys because they have little waste. A Porterhouse steak will usually give two servings per pound, while a rib eye roast will give three."

Beef supplies high-quality, complete protein, containing all eight amino acids required by our bodies for growth, maintenance, and repair. One three-ounce cooked serving of beef will supply about 50 percent of the protein recommended daily for most people. Beef also contains significant amounts of vitamin B_2, niacin, vitamin B_{12}, iron, and zinc.

Before you buy it, all meat is inspected for wholesomeness. At the supermarket, look for a bright to deep red color on lean beef and small flecks of fat, called marbling. Don't worry if packaged ground beef looks darker in the inside. Beef is dark purplish-red when first cut, but becomes bright red when exposed to oxygen in the air.

You can store packaged and wrapped beef in the refrigerator for two to four days, but if you don't intend to use it soon, freeze it while it's freshest. For a short storage time—up to two weeks—you can freeze it just as it comes prepacked from the meat counter. For longer periods, carefully overwrap each package in freezer paper. Then it'll keep well for several months.

Beef
in the Menu

BARBECUE DINNER PARTY

Red and White Wine

Cheese and Crackers   Guacamole Grande** with
Tortilla Chips

California Pinot Noir

Flank Steak Roll*

Foil-Wrapped French Bread and Butter

Avocado Caesar Salad**

Berry Elegant Pie***

Coffee or Tea

*See Beef Recipes
**See Avocado Recipes
***See Strawberry Recipes

Fiesta Beef

1½ pounds ground beef
6 tablespoons dry bread crumbs
⅔ cup (4 oz.) onion, chopped
1 teaspoon salt
1 teaspoon chili powder
¼ teaspoon pepper
½ cup (4 fl. oz.) milk
1 avocado, peeled and seeded
4 small sticks (2 oz.) Cheddar cheese
1 tomato, cut in quarters
½ cup (4 fl. oz.) sour cream

Preheat oven to 375° F. (190° C.).

Combine beef, bread crumbs, onion, salt, chili powder, pepper, and milk in bowl; mix well. Divide beef into eight balls and pat balls into oblong patties. Cut avocado lengthwise into four parts. Put a piece of avocado, a stick of cheese, and a tomato wedge on a beef patty. Cover with a second beef patty and pinch edges well to enclose filling. Repeat to make remaining servings.

Put filled loaves on a shallow baking sheet and bake for 25 to 30 minutes, or until browned. To serve, top with dollops of sour cream.

Swedish Meat Balls

1 pound ground beef
¼ pound ground pork
1 egg
1 teaspoon salt
½ teaspoon pepper
1 onion, chopped

¼ teaspoon allspice
3 or 4 slices bread, crumbled
1 cup (8 fl. oz.) milk
2 tablespoons butter
3 tablespoons all-purpose flour
1½ cups (12 fl. oz.) beef stock

Combine beef, pork, egg, salt, pepper, onion, allspice, bread crumbs, and milk. Form mixture into small balls. Melt butter in a pan and fry meatballs until browned but still slightly pink inside. Remove from pan. Pour off all but 3 tablespoons fat. Add flour to pan and cook for 2 minutes, stirring constantly. Add stock and cook, stirring, until a thick gravy is formed. Return meatballs to pan and simmer until fully cooked.

Barbequed Brisket

1 beef brisket, 4 to 7 pounds
4 tablespoons soy sauce
1½ cups (12 fl. oz.) beef consommé
1 tablespoon Worcestershire sauce
1 tablespoon vinegar
1 tablespoon liquid smoke flavoring
1 clove garlic, chopped

Preheat oven to 300° F. (150° C.).

Place meat in a deep dish. Combine soy sauce, consommé, Worcestershire sauce, vinegar, smoke flavoring, and garlic. Pour mixture over meat and marinate for 24 hours. Bake in ungreased pan, covered, for 4 or 5 hours, or until tender. Slice and serve.

Chili Verde

Meat mixture:

2 pounds beef stew meat, cubed
1 cup (8 fl. oz.) water
2 teaspoons salt
2 tablespoons butter
2 tablespoons olive oil
3 large tomatoes, peeled and chopped
4 to 6 fresh chilis, minced
1 onion, minced
2 cloves garlic, mashed
8 large flour or corn tortillas

Garnish:

4 cups (16 oz.) lettuce, shredded
1 cup (8 oz.) tomatoes, chopped
1 cup (6 oz.) green onions, chopped
2 cups (16 fl. oz.) sour cream
2 cups (16 fl. oz.) salsa (optional)

Place meat in a pan with the water and salt. Cover and cook slowly until meat is tender and water is absorbed. Add more water, if necessary. Melt butter, add oil, and brown meat. Add tomatoes, chilis, onion, and garlic. Simmer for 20 minutes, or until flavors are combined.

To serve, spoon meat mixture onto tortillas. Garnish with lettuce, tomatoes, green onions, sour cream, and salsa, if used.

Shortribs in Beer

¼ cup (1¼ oz.) all-purpose flour
1 teaspoon salt
¼ teaspoon pepper
4 pounds beef ribs, cut in 3-inch (8-cm.) pieces
¼ cup (2 fl. oz.) butter
2 onions, chopped
¼ cup (3 fl. oz.) molasses
½ cup (4 fl. oz.) catsup
2 tablespoons brown sugar
½ tablespoon Tabasco sauce (optional)
3 tablespoons vinegar
¾ cup (6 fl. oz.) beer
6 carrots, peeled and cut in thirds
salt and pepper, to taste

Combine flour, salt, and pepper. Coat ribs with this mixture. In a heavy pan, melt butter, add ribs, and brown on all sides. Remove. Add onions and cook until tender. Add molasses, catsup, brown sugar, Tabasco sauce (if used), vinegar, beer, and browned ribs. Simmer for 1½ to 2 hours. Remove ribs, skim off fat, and return ribs to pan. Add carrots, salt, and pepper and cook until tender, 15 to 20 minutes.

Beefsteak Parmesan

Grated cheese forms a savory coating for this tasty barbecued beef.

1 to 1¼ pounds boneless top sirloin, cut ¾ to 1-inch
    (2 to 2½-cm.) thick
3 tablespoons olive oil
⅓ cup (2⅔ fl. oz.) dry red wine
2 tablespoons chili sauce
¼ teaspoon garlic, minced
¼ teaspoon salt
¼ teaspoon pepper
½ cup (2 oz.) Parmesan cheese, finely grated

Prepare barbecue.

Cut beef into 4 equal servings. Combine oil, wine, chili sauce, garlic, salt, and pepper; pour liquid over beef and marinate for 4 hours or overnight. Remove beef from marinade, drain, and coat with cheese. Place steaks about 3-inches (8-cm.) above hot coals; barbecue 5 to 6 minutes on one side, turn steaks, sprinkle generously with cheese, barbecue 5 minutes on second side.

Creole Steak Strips

1½ pounds boneless round steak, cut into 2-inch
    (5-cm.) strips
salt and pepper, to taste
1 onion, chopped
1 cup (6 oz.) celery, sliced
1 cup (8 fl. oz.) tomato juice
2 teaspoons Worcestershire sauce
⅛ teaspoon garlic powder
1 green pepper, chopped

1½ cups (9 oz.) okra
½ cup (1½ oz.) mushrooms, sliced
3 cups (8 oz.) cooked rice, hot
carrot curls, as needed

Place steak in a slow-cooking pot. Sprinkle with salt and pepper. Add onion, celery, tomato juice, Worcestershire sauce, and garlic powder. Cover and cook on low power for 6 to 8 hours. Add green pepper, okra, and mushrooms, and cook on high for 30 minutes. To serve, spoon over rice and garnish with carrot curls.

Beef and Asparagus Beijing

3 cups (1 lb.) fresh asparagus, trimmed and cut
    into ½-inch (1½-cm.) pieces
2 onions, cut into narrow wedges
2 cloves garlic, minced
2 tablespoons soy sauce
2 tablespoons sherry
1 teaspoon sugar
½ teaspoon ground ginger
4 tablespoons vegetable oil
1 pound beef, cut across grain into thin slices
3 cups (8 oz.) cooked rice, hot

Place asparagus, onions, and garlic in a bowl. Combine soy sauce, sherry, sugar, and ginger and pour over asparagus mixture. Heat 2 tablespoons oil in a heavy skillet or wok. Add asparagus mixture and cook, stirring, over high heat for 3 minutes. In another pan, heat remaining oil and cook beef over high heat for 2 or 3 minutes, until brown on outside but still medium-rare inside. Add to asparagus. To serve, mound on rice.

Flank Steak Roll

4 slices bacon, chopped
1 onion, minced
2 cups (6 oz.) mushrooms, sliced
3 slices bread, cubed
½ bunch parsley, chopped
⅓ cup (2⅔ fl. oz.) catsup
½ teaspoon lemon juice
2 tablespoons brown sugar
1 or 2 drops of liquid smoke flavoring
1½ teaspoons soy sauce
1 teaspoon salt
1 teaspoon pepper
1 teaspoon dry mustard
⅓ cup (2⅔ fl. oz.) vegetable oil
⅓ cup (2⅔ fl. oz.) olive oil
2 flank steaks, butterflied
6 slices Jack or mild Cheddar cheese

Prepare barbecue.

Fry bacon. Remove from pan with a slotted spoon and drain on a towel. In bacon fat, sauté onion and mushrooms. Remove from pan and toss with bread and parsley long enough to wilt parsley. Set aside.

In a saucepan, combine catsup, lemon juice, brown sugar, smoke flavoring, soy sauce, salt, pepper, and mustard. Bring mixture to boil and remove from heat. Stir in vegetable oil and olive oil.

Open flank steaks and baste with oil mixture. Spread mushroom mixture to within 1-inch (2½-cm.) of edges. Place cheese on top and carefully roll each steak. Tie with string. Barbecue over low coals for 45 minutes, basting frequently.

Roast Beef Normandy

2 cups (16 fl. oz.) apple cider or juice
½ cup (4 fl. oz.) brandy
1 teaspoon lemon peel, grated
1 sirloin tip roast, 3 to 4 pounds
2 onions, cut into wedges
2 apples, cut into wedges
4 teaspoons all-purpose flour
½ cup (4 fl. oz.) heavy cream
½ teaspoon salt
dash nutmeg
dash cinnamon

Combine apple cider or juice, brandy, and lemon peel in a bowl. Add beef, cover, and marinate in the refrigerator for several hours or overnight. Preheat oven to 375° F. (190° C.). Lift beef from marinade and place with onions and ½ cup (4 fl. oz.) marinade in a roasting pan. Roast for ½ hour. Add apple wedges to roasting pan. Roast 2 hours longer or until beef registers 135° F. (57° C.) (for medium-rare) on a meat thermometer.

Meanwhile, pour remaining marinade into a saucepan, bring to a boil, and cook until reduced to about 1 cup (8 fl. oz.).

When cooked as desired, arrange beef, onions, and apples on a serving platter. Strain meat juices into marinade. Skim off fat. Blend flour with 2 tablespoons water, and add to reduced marinade in saucepan. Cook over medium heat until sauce thickens slightly. Stir in cream, salt, nutmeg, and cinnamon. Heat through and serve with roast.

21 | CHICKEN
The Calorie Counter's
Ray of Sunshine

Napoleon's cook once won a bet that he could prepare a different but delicious chicken dish for each of the 365 days of the year. Poultry farmers enjoy this little piece of history, since they too believe that chicken is almost infinite in its versatility. Just a tiny change in seasonings or cooking methods can create an entirely different taste sensation.

Poultry farmers have other reasons to be happy with their product as well. "Chicken is a calorie counter's ray of sunshine," says an enthusiastic Joan Riebli, wife of poultry farmer Arnold Riebli. "A three-ounce portion of skinless broiled chicken breast contains only 115 calories, and even with the skin left on, the calorie count is only 185. An equivalent size serving of roast pork," she says by way of contrast, "is 310 calories, and hamburger has 245 calories." Also, that 115 calories of chicken supplies a whopping 23 grams of protein.

Joan likes to point out that chicken is a real help to people on low-fat diets too. Although no meat is lower in fat content than chicken, there is an even more beneficial aspect; the fatty acids contained in chicken are two-thirds unsaturated. Further, chicken fat contains a higher proportion of linoleic acid than most other animal fats.

Linoleic acid is important, partly because it is necessary for growth and reproduction, but also because, when it constitutes 25 percent or more of the fat consumed, linoleic acid lowers blood cholesterol in adults under certain dietary conditions.

If you are dieting, choose the chicken breast and remove the skin. Six ounces of chicken breast contains only about 3 grams of fat, while an equivalent amount of chicken thigh contains more than 7 grams of fat, and the same amount of chicken wing contains more than 6 grams. Fat is more fattening than protein.

What about flavor? Would you guess that the chicken of Grandmother's time was tastier? The Department of Agriculture wondered the same thing and arranged a clever test to find out. A panel of tasters was asked to compare the flavor of modern chickens with birds of 1930 breeding stock that had been fed 1930s' rations. After tasting the two sets of broilers cooked in a number of ways, the panelists could not detect any difference in flavor between the modern ones and the old-fashioned ones.

There is one difference between today's birds and those of half a century ago. At that time, birds were usually marketed at about sixteen weeks of age, while today's broilers are ready for market at seven to nine weeks. Older birds have the same flavor as the younger ones, but the flavor is stronger. If you want a more intense chicken flavor, choose a roaster, or any bird weighing from 3.5 to 6 pounds. The heavier weight indicates older age and stronger flavor.

Soup and stew manufacturers know this secret, and they are the prime buyers for old laying hens. A laying hen would be too tough and lean for roasting or frying, but it gives a dandy taste to stew.

The flavor of the 1930s breeding stock might be undistinguishable from today's supermarket bird, but it is nevertheless a very different bird. The 1930s' bird required 4.5 pounds of feed to produce 1 pound of live chicken. Today, through advances in genetics and nutrition, the poultry farmer can produce the same pound of chicken for only 2 pounds of feed. "In fact," says Arnold Riebli, "chicken is the most efficient machine known for converting grain into protein."

When shopping for chicken—and you do so often if you're like most Americans, who eat 48 pounds of it a year—here's what you'll find at the supermarket: the small (under 1.5 pounds) specially bred Rock Cornish hen; the 2- to 3.5-pound broiler-fryer; and the 3.5- to 6-pound roaster. Occasionally a larger stewing bird is available, too. Usually not more than two or three days have elapsed between processing and delivery to your market.

Chicken should be stored in the coldest part of the refrigerator. If you won't be using it within two days, wrap it tightly in foil or freezer paper, seal, and freeze. Properly packaged frozen chicken will maintain its flavor for up to six months. Left-over cooked chicken should be stored refrigerated and eaten within a day or two.

You, too, could cook with chicken 365 days a year and never repeat a recipe. It is one of our most versatile meats.

Chicken
in the Menu

SUPPER

Beer   Sweet-and-Sour
Chicken Tidbits*

Avocado Caesar Salad**

Crusty French Bread and Butter

Green-Noodle Tetrazzini*

New England Apple Sauce Cake***

Coffee or Tea

*See Chicken Recipes
**See Avocado Recipes
***See Apple Recipes

Sweet-and-Sour Chicken Tidbits

1 pound chicken wings
½ cup (4 fl. oz.) white wine vinegar
½ cup (4 fl. oz.) pineapple juice
¼ cup (2 fl. oz.) catsup
¼ cup (1¾ oz.) sugar
2 tablespoons soy sauce
1 tablespoon cornstarch
3 tablespoons toasted sesame seeds
½ teaspoon salt

Cut off wing tips and cut each wing in half at main joint. Place in a baking dish. In a saucepan, combine vinegar, pineapple juice, catsup, sugar, soy sauce, and cornstarch. Bring to a boil and boil for 2 minutes. Pour sauce over chicken. Marinate at room temperature for 1 hour.

Preheat oven to 400° F. (205° C.). Bake chicken for 45 minutes, turning occasionally. Combine sesame seeds and salt in a shallow dish. Roll each chicken wing in sesame seeds and serve.

Orange Baked Chicken Appetizers

1 pound chicken wings
½ cup (4 fl. oz.) orange juice
¼ cup (3 fl. oz.) honey
¼ cup (1½ oz.) onion, finely chopped
2 teaspoons Dijon mustard
1 teaspoon orange rind, finely grated
¼ teaspoon tarragon
⅛ teaspoon salt
2 oranges, thinly sliced

Cut off wing tips and cut wings in half at main joint. Place in a shallow dish. In a saucepan, mix orange juice, honey, onion, mustard, orange rind, tarragon, and salt. Bring sauce to a boil and boil 2 minutes. Pour over chicken and marinate for 2 to 3 hours, turning once. Preheat oven to 350° F. (180° C.). Place chicken on a rack in a baking dish. Brush with sauce. Bake for 40 minutes.

To serve, garnish with orange slices.

Lemon Fricasseed Chicken

1½ pounds chicken pieces, cut up
salt and pepper, to taste
2 tablespoons vegetable oil
1 cup (8 fl. oz.) chicken broth
¼ cup (2 fl. oz.) dry white wine
¾ cup (6 fl. oz.) sour cream
2 egg yolks, slightly beaten
2 tablespoons lemon juice
½ teaspoon salt
¼ teaspoon dill weed
¼ teaspoon pepper
3 to 4 cups (8 oz.) noodles, cooked and hot
chopped parsley, as needed

Pat chicken pieces dry. Season with salt and pepper. Heat oil in a large skillet. Sauté chicken pieces until lightly browned. Drain off oil. Add broth and wine, cover, and simmer for 30 minutes. In a small bowl, combine sour cream, egg yolks, lemon juice, salt, dill weed, and pepper. Slowly stir into skillet, and heat for 5 minutes, or until slightly thickened. Do not allow to boil.

To serve, mound chicken and sauce over noodles. Garnish with parsley.

Chicken Crêpe Cake

Sauce:

> 3 tablespoons butter
> 3 tablespoons all-purpose flour
> 1½ cups (12 fl. oz.) milk
> ¼ teaspoon salt
> ⅛ teaspoon pepper
> ⅛ teaspoon nutmeg

Melt butter in a saucepan. Blend in flour and cook, stirring for 1 minute. Add milk and cook, stirring, until smooth. Add salt, pepper, and nutmeg and simmer for 10 minutes.

Filling:

> 3 tablespoons butter
> 2 cups (12 oz.) spinach, cooked and chopped
> ⅓ cup (1½ oz.) Parmesan cheese, grated
> ¼ teaspoon salt
> ⅛ teaspoon pepper
> ⅛ teaspoon nutmeg
> 12 to 14 entrée crêpes, cooked
> 1½ cups (12 oz.) chicken, cooked and diced
> ⅓ cup (2 oz.) Swiss cheese, grated

Preheat oven to 375° F. (190° C.).

Melt butter in a saucepan. Stir in spinach, Parmesan cheese, salt, pepper, and nutmeg. Cook over low heat, stirring constantly, for 3 minutes.

To assemble crêpe cake, lightly butter a 10-inch (25-cm.) pie plate and place a crêpe on bottom. Spread with one-sixth of the chicken. Top with another crêpe. Spread with one-sixth of the spinach filling. Repeat layers, ending with a crêpe. Pour sauce over the top and sprinkle with Swiss cheese. Bake for 15 minutes. Place under a hot broiler and broil until sauce is lightly browned. To serve, cut into wedges.

Green-Noodle Tetrazzini

3 to 4 cups (8 oz.) spinach noodles
salt, as needed
3 cups (24 oz.) chicken, cooked and diced
2 cups (6 oz.) mushrooms, sliced
¼ cup (2 fl. oz.) butter
½ teaspoon basil
½ teaspoon oregano
½ teaspoon salt
½ teaspoon pepper
2 cloves garlic, crushed
¼ cup (1¼ oz.) all-purpose flour
1 cup (8 fl. oz.) chicken stock
1 cup (8 fl. oz.) heavy cream
¼ cup (2 fl. oz.) dry sherry
¼ cup (1 oz.) Parmesan cheese, grated

Preheat oven to 350° F. (180° C.).

Cook noodles in boiling, salted water until tender, about 8 minutes. Drain. Mix with chicken and mushrooms and set aside. In a saucepan, melt butter and sauté basil, oregano, salt, pepper, and garlic for 2 minutes. Blend in flour and cook, stirring, for 1 minute. Slowly stir in stock, cream, and sherry and stir until smooth. Place noodle mixture in a shallow 2-quart (64-oz.) baking dish, pour sauce over and sprinkle with Parmesan cheese. Bake for 45 minutes.

Chicken Blossom Salad

Salad:

   3 cups (24 oz.) chicken, cooked and cubed
   1 cup (6 oz.) Mandarin oranges
   ⅔ cup (4 oz.) water chestnuts, sliced
   ½ cup (3 oz.) celery, diced
   2 green onions, sliced
   lettuce, as needed

Combine chicken, oranges, water chestnuts, celery, and green onions. Line four chilled plates with lettuce leaves and mound one-quarter of mixture on each plate.

Dressing:

   ¼ cup (2 fl. oz.) cider vinegar
   1 egg yolk
   1 tablespoon sugar
   1 teaspoon dry mustard
   ¾ teaspoon salt
   ½ teaspoon ground ginger
   ¾ cup (6 fl. oz.) vegetable oil

Place vinegar, egg yolk, sugar, mustard, salt, and ginger in a blender container. Cover and run on high speed for 1 minute. Add oil and blend until smooth and thick.

   To serve, pour dressing over salad mixture. Chill 2 hours before serving.

Poached Chicken

Chicken:

> 1 whole chicken
> water, as needed
> 1 stalk celery, halved
> 1 carrot, peeled and halved
> 1 onion, halved
> 1 teaspoon salt
> 4 sprigs parsley
> 1 bay leaf
> 2 whole cloves
> ½ teaspoon thyme

Preheat crock pot to low or oven to 325° F. (165° C.).

Place chicken in a crock pot or large casserole and cover with water. Add celery, carrot, onion, and salt. Tie parsley, bay leaf, cloves, and thyme in a small square of cheesecloth. Add to water, cover and cook in a crock pot on low for 7 to 9 hours or in oven for 1½ hours, or until tender.

Sauce:

> 6 tablespoons butter
> ¼ cup (1¼ oz.) all-purpose flour
> 1 cup (8 fl. oz.) chicken broth
> ⅛ teaspoon pepper
> ¼ cup (1 oz.) parsley, chopped
> ½ cup (4 fl. oz.) heavy cream

Melt 4 tablespoons of the butter in a saucepan. Stir in flour and cook over low heat for 2 minutes. Add broth and cook until thickened. Add pepper, parsley, and cream. Just before serving, slowly beat in remaining 2 tablespoons butter.

Slice chicken, and serve with creamy sauce.

Curried Chicken

1½ pounds chicken pieces, cut up
salt and pepper, to taste
1 tablespoon curry powder
2 tablespoons butter
2 tablespoons vegetable oil
½ cup (3 oz.) onion, chopped
1½ cups (12 fl. oz.) chicken broth
½ cup (3 oz.) apple, peeled and finely chopped
2 tablespoons cornstarch
¼ cup (2 fl. oz.) heavy cream
2 to 3 cups (6 to 9 oz.) rice, cooked and hot
2 bananas, sliced
½ cup (2½ oz.) raisins
2 eggs, hard-boiled and chopped
½ cup (2 oz.) almonds, slivered

Pat chicken pieces dry. Season with salt, pepper, and curry powder. Melt butter and oil in a large skillet. Add chicken and onion and sauté until chicken is lightly browned. Add broth and apples, bring to a boil, and simmer, covered, for 30 minutes. Combine cornstarch and cream. Stir into chicken and cook until thickened.

To serve, mound chicken and sauce over rice. Serve with bananas, raisins, egg, and almonds.

22 | LAMB
The Aftershave Connection

Would it surprise you to know there's a new and exciting connection between the lamb you buy in the supermarket and ... aftershave lotion?

There is, and here's how it works. When a baby lamb is orphaned, or when a ewe gives birth to triplets or quadruplets and can't feed them all adequately, the lambs are apt to starve. In the past, 10 percent of all the lambs born in this country died of starvation. Another ewe will not nurse orphan babies even when she has milk to spare since Mother Nature has programmed her not to suckle a stranger's infant, and she can smell when a baby lamb is not hers.

For centuries, shepherds have been trying to "graft" starving lambs onto ewes with extra milk. Making a ewe think the orphan is hers by tying the skin of the dead lamb onto the "graft" baby, or smearing the afterbirth of the dead lamb over the orphaned lamb sometimes works. But these methods are chancy and only work well for newborns.

Today, aftershave lotion might be offering a better solution. When shepherds douse a baby lamb with aftershave and then sprinkle a goodly amount on a ewe's nose, the ewe can't use odor to tell whether the baby is hers or not and won't push the little stranger away. Aftershave, then, is important to the sheep industry. (But so are Scotch and deodorant, which work equally well.)

Ewes might be good at pushing away strangers' babies, but they are singularly poor at recognizing their own babies. One of the most important attributes of a good shepherd is that he must have *oreja*—that's Spanish for "ear"—because it takes *oreja* to put the right mother with the right baby. Doris Indart, wife and mother of sheep ranchers, explains. "Ewes are no better at sorting out their babies than human mothers would be in the same situation. Imagine one hundred human mothers giving birth in the same dark room at night, and imagine that all their babies could get up and toddle off right after they were born." Mrs. Indart shakes her head at the mere thought of such chaos.

"If the mothers don't find their lambs, the lambs will starve. A good ear is important"—you can almost hear the tenderness in Mrs. Indart's voice—"because a shepherd who 'has ear' can match up the mothers and babies, even in the dark, by the sound of their bleats."

The lambing season lasts from mid-October to mid-February, and, as sheep rancher Oscar Durst remarks, "It takes a dedicated person to work during the lambing season. It's seven-days-a-week, around-the-clock work."

A shepherd's work is exacting even when it isn't lambing season. He must be almost constantly on the watch for coyotes. In 1977, 534,000 lambs were slaughtered by coyotes, and in 1978, coyotes killed more than $40 million worth of lambs. "There's only one month of the year when coyotes don't bother us," sighs Durst, "and that's when the deer drop their fawns. A fawn is even more defenseless than a baby lamb."

Predators inevitably increase the cost of lamb at our supermarkets, but even so, sheep have a lot going for them. As Michele Howard, Executive Vice President of the California Wool Growers Association, puts it, "Sheep lead all agriculture in terms of energy efficiency—the conversion of unprocessed feed into both meat and fiber. They can utilize ground unsuitable for crops and which can't be used by any other animals except maybe goats."

What about lamb and nutrition? "Lamb is an excellent source of protein, thiamine, riboflavin, niacin, and minerals such as iron and zinc," says Howard, "and a 3-ounce serving of roast leg of lamb gives only 158 calories, while contributing 40 percent of the United States Recommended Daily Allowance for protein."

And how about selecting lamb at the supermarket? First of all, don't look for "spring lamb" anymore—*all* lamb you'll find is between five and seven months old, and due to the variety of production sites, it's now available all year round. Since lamb is young, the meat is lean and smooth, and should be a healthy rosy color.

Perhaps you've noticed that there's a better meat-to-bone ratio on lamb than in former years. That's because genetics and better production practices have created a much meatier animal.

Donna Hamilton, of the American Lamb Council, points out that lamb is a natural for dieters. "It's naturally portion controlled," she exults. "Each chop contains 3 to 3.5 ounces of tender lean meat." Economical, too, since you don't over-purchase.

Donna Hamilton stresses the correct way to prepare lamb. "Always cook it at a slow—325 degrees Fahrenheit (165 degrees Celsius)—temperature until it's lightly pink inside (it should measure 145 degreees Fahrenheit [63 degrees Celsius] on a meat thermometer). And if you're roasting, don't remove the fell, the parchment-like outer covering. It'll hold in the juices and give you a tender, moist treat."

Oscar Durst believes that barbecued lamb is so tasty that there's nothing to be gained by adding any seasonings beyond salt and pepper. He especially likes boned shoulder of lamb and feels that most consumers aren't sufficiently aware of this cut. "It's not the tenderest cut, but it's not the most expensive either. And what's good about it is— it's one tasty piece of meat!"

Try it next time you barbecue!

Lamb
in the Menu

LUNCH

California Rosé

Corn and Tomato Chowder**

Lamb Salad*
Whole Wheat Rolls and Butter

Dutch Almond Cookies***

Fresh Fruit

Coffee or Tea

*See Lamb Recipes
**See Corn Recipes
***See Almond Recipes

Lamb Salad

1½ cups (12 fl. oz.) cups water
¾ teaspoon salt
¾ cup (6 oz.) brown rice
2 cups (16 oz.) cooked lamb, chopped
3 stalks celery, chopped
3 green onions, chopped
½ cup (2 oz.) toasted sunflower seeds
1 cup (8 fl. oz.) mayonnaise
½ cup (4 fl. oz.) catsup
2 tablespoons lemon juice
salt and pepper, to taste
2 avocados, halved, or 2 halved papayas, or 1 quartered pineapple
lettuce leaves, as needed

Bring water and salt to a boil. Add rice, cover, and cook for 45 minutes, or until tender. Cool.

In a large bowl, combine rice, lamb, celery, onion, and sunflower seeds. In a small bowl, combine mayonnaise, catsup, lemon juice, salt, and pepper. Fold dressing into lamb mixture. Chill.

For each serving, mound salad mixture on an avocado half, or a half papaya, or a quarter pineapple, and place on lettuce leaf.

Lamb and Bean Bake

1 cup (8 oz.) small white beans
3 tablespoons vegetable oil
1 pound lamb shoulder, cubed
1 onion, chopped
1 clove garlic, minced

1 cup (6 oz.) celery, chopped
1 cup (6 oz.) carrots, chopped
1 cup (8 oz.) tomatoes, chopped
½ teaspoon oregano
salt and pepper, to taste

Soak beans in water overnight. Drain. In a heavy casserole, lightly brown in oil the lamb, onions, and garlic. Add beans, celery, carrots, tomatoes, oregano, salt, and pepper. Add water to barely cover. Simmer, covered, for at least 3 hours, or until tender.

Excellent served with corn muffins.

Chilindron

This Chilindron is an old and rather unique Basque recipe that is highly recommended by the family of a California lamb grower.

2 pounds lamb, stew meat or riblets
½ cup (2½ oz.) all-purpose flour
½ cup (4 fl. oz.) vegetable oil
1 onion, minced
2 cloves garlic, minced
salt and pepper, to taste
½ cup (4 fl. oz.) white wine
1 large dried red pimiento
1 cup (8 oz.) tomatoes, chopped

Coat lamb with flour and brown in a large casserole in hot oil. Remove lamb from casserole. Add onion and garlic and brown in some oil. Return meat to casserole. Season with salt and pepper. Add wine, pimiento, and tomatoes. Cover and cook until tender, approximately 2 hours.

Baked Lamb Shanks

4 lamb shanks
1 onion, chopped
2 carrots, sliced
2 potatoes, quartered
2 tomatoes, quartered
salt and pepper, to taste
1 cup (8 fl. oz.) red wine

Preheat oven to 325° F. (165° C.).

Combine lamb, onion, carrots, potatoes, tomatoes, salt, pepper, and wine in a covered baking dish. Bake for 1½ to 2 hours, or until thoroughly tender. Remove cover and brown under broiler for 10 minutes.

Shish Kabob

1 leg of lamb, 5 to 6 pounds
2 large onions, cut in wedges
2 green peppers, cut in wedges
1 cup (4 oz.) fresh parsley, minced
½ cup (4 fl. oz.) red wine
2 tablespoons lemon juice
½ cup (4 fl. oz.) olive oil
salt and pepper, to taste

Cut lamb into 2-inch cubes. In a large bowl, combine onions, peppers, parsley, wine, lemon juice, and olive oil. Add lamb and marinate for at least 3 hours.

Prepare barbecue.

Spear lamb, onions, and peppers alternately on skewers. Sprinkle with salt and pepper. Cook over coals to desired degree of doneness.

Ground-Lamb Casserole

1 pound ground lamb
1 cup (6 oz.) onion, chopped
½ cup (2 oz.) fresh parsley, chopped
½ teaspoon sweet basil leaves, crushed
salt and pepper, to taste
1 medium eggplant, zucchini, or summer squash
1 tablespoon olive oil
1 tomato, sliced
1 green pepper, sliced
½ teaspoon garlic salt
1 cup (4 oz.) Parmesan cheese, grated

Preheat oven to 350° F. (180° C.).

In a pan, brown ground lamb with onion, parsley, and sweet basil. Drain excess fat. Season with salt and pepper.

Cut eggplant, zucchini, or summer squash into ⅛-inch (½-cm.) slices. Arrange half the vegetable slices in a single layer in an oiled shallow baking dish. Spoon cooked meat mixture over vegetable slices and cover with remaining vegetable slices. Brush with oil. Layer tomato and pepper slices on top. Season with garlic salt. Sprinkle Parmesan cheese over all. Cover casserole with foil and bake for 45 minutes. Remove foil and bake for another 15 minutes.

23 | PORK
Penny–Wise Pigs

"A pig isn't really a pig," insists pretty Janet Wolter, wife of a hog rancher. "A pig is one of the few animals you can name that won't make a pig of itself by overeating if given the chance. A horse or cow will eat itself sick, but a pig knows just when to stop."

Another myth about pigs is that they're dirty. Because pigs have no sweat glands, they used to like to wallow in mud to keep cool. But today's pigs often live in special temperature-controlled, ultra-sanitary "pig parlors," where they are kept clean and their diets watched.

In fact, pigs are in many ways quite different from the stereotypes we have of them. Hog ranchers are concerned that many consumers might not realize how much pork has changed in the last generation. Years ago, when hogs were raised mainly for the lard they provided, a market hog might weigh 300 to 400 pounds or more. Today, the average hog is sold at between 220 to 240 pounds. If the animal is even a few pounds over the ideal weight, the rancher will be penalized for an animal that might have too much fat.

Genetic research has also helped produce a leaner animal. That together with modern feeding practices and the selling of younger animals means that today's pig contains 22 percent more protein and 57 percent less fat than pigs of a few years ago.

On top of that, today's pork contains 36 percent fewer calories than the pork of a few years ago. It's even recommended in the major weight reduction programs—Weight Watchers International and Diet Workshop.

Pork is also more digestible than it used to be. According to the National Pork Producers Council, today's pork is 96 percent to 98 percent digestible, one of the highest ratings given for any food.

Today's leaner pork should be cooked differently than the old-style pork. Barbara Chittenden, a hog rancher and a spokesperson for the Porkettes says, "You'd be surprised how many of the current cookbooks are out of date!" Barbara makes a point of checking cookbooks in bookstores, and is disconcerted by how often she finds them still recommending that pork be cooked to an internal temperature of 185 degrees Fahrenheit (85 degrees Celsius). "But we in the industry know that pork gets tough at that temperature and loses some of its delicious flavor. If you want it tenderer, juicier, and with a very special flavor, take your roast from the oven when it's reached 170 degrees Fahrenheit (77 degrees Celsius). And don't worry about harmful organisms surviving at this lower temperature," adds Barbara. "Scientists have determined that pork is safe to eat at 140 degrees Fahrenheit."

What about pork and nutrition? Pork is the richest food source of vitamin B-1 (thiamin) you can find. It contains three times as much as any other food. Vitamin B-1 is essential for using carbohydrates to produce energy. Without enough of this vitamin, people tire easily and experience general weakness. It's also important for a healthy central nervous system and a good mental attitude.

Pork is also high in iron, riboflavin, niacin, phosphorus, magnesium, and more.

At the supermarket, look for fresh, pink cuts of pork with some visible flecks of fat. At home, refrigerate immediately for up to two days. For longer storage, wrap in freezer paper and freeze for up to six months.

Today's leaner, meatier pork is economical—one of the best meat buys around. When purchasing pork, it's the price per serving that counts. One-quarter pound of boneless pork, one-third pound of pork chop, and three-quarters pound of pork spareribs are each equal to one serving.

But whatever forms you buy, today's pork will be a tasty treat.

Pork
in the Menu

BARBECUED DINNER

Wine or Beer

Pork-Stuffed Appetizer Mushrooms*

South Pacific Pork Kabobs*

Fresh Pineapple Chunks

Salted Peanuts

Foil-Wrapped Bread and Butter

Avocado and Shrimp Salad**

Strawberries Romanoff***

Coffee or Tea

*See Pork Recipes
**See Avocado Recipes
***See Strawberry Recipes

Aunt Carole's Chili

3 cups (1½ lb.) pinto beans
2 pounds pork sausage
6 tomatoes, peeled, seeded, and chopped
½ bell pepper, chopped
½ onion, chopped
2 cloves garlic, crushed
½ cup (2 oz.) parsley, chopped
¼ teaspoon chili powder
salt, to taste
1½ teaspoons pepper
1½ teaspoons monosodium glutamate
1½ teaspoons cumin
water, as needed to cover

Wash and soak beans overnight. Drain. Place in a large casserole. In a frying pan, brown sausage. Drain, and add to beans. Add tomatoes, pepper, onion, garlic, parsley, chili powder, salt, pepper, monosodium glutamate, cumin, and water. Cook slowly, covered, until beans are tender. Alternatively, may be cooked in a crock pot on high for 6 to 7 hours.

Pork-Stuffed Appetizer Mushrooms

½ pound ground pork
1 egg, beaten
½ cup (3 oz.) onions, finely chopped
½ cup (2 oz.) soft bread crumbs
⅛ teaspoon nutmeg
salt and pepper, to taste
20 medium mushroom caps
½ cup (4 fl. oz.) yogurt

In a medium bowl, combine ground pork, egg, onion, bread

crumbs, nutmeg, salt, and pepper. Shape pork mixture into 20 balls. Place pork balls on rack in broiler pan. Broil 3 to 4 inches (8 to 10 cm.) from heat until browned, about 5 minutes, turn; broil until pork balls are done, about 5 minutes. Keep warm. Place mushroom caps on rack in broiler pan. Broil 3 to 4 inches (8 to 10 cm.) from heat until heated through, about 2 minutes. Spear pork balls with wooden picks and place inside or on top of mushroom caps. Spoon about 1 teaspoon yogurt on top of each appetizer. Serve at once.

Pork Curry

1½ pounds lean boneless pork, cubed
¼ cup (1¼ oz.) all-purpose flour
3 tablespoons vegetable oil
1 or more tablespoons curry powder, to taste
1 medium onion, sliced
1 clove garlic, finely minced
1 apple, chopped
1 cup (8 fl. oz.) beef stock
¼ cup (2 fl. oz.) tomato paste
1 teaspoon light brown sugar
½ teaspoon salt
¼ teaspoon dry mustard
¼ teaspoon ginger
1½ cups (9 oz.) green peas

Coat meat in flour. Brown lightly in oil. Add curry powder, onion, and garlic and cook until soft. Add apple, beef stock, tomato paste, sugar, salt, mustard, and ginger. Mix well, cover, and simmer gently for 1½ hours, or until meat is fork tender. Add peas and cook for 10 minutes.

May be served over rice, accompanied by chopped nuts, chutney, and pineapple chunks.

Pork Chop and Potato Bake

6 medium potatoes
salt and pepper, to taste
2 tablespoons vegetable oil
4 pork chops
¼ cup (2 fl. oz.) butter
¼ cup (1¼ oz.) all-purpose flour
2½ cups (20 fl. oz.) milk

Preheat oven to 350° F. (180° C.).

Scrub potatoes and slice thinly with peel left on. Place in a large casserole. Add salt and pepper. Toss lightly with a fork.

Place oil in a frying pan and brown pork chops over medium heat. Remove chops from pan and place on top of potatoes. Season with salt and pepper.

In the same pan, melt butter. Add flour and cook for 1 minute. Slowly add milk and cook until sauce thickens. Pour over potatoes. Cover tightly and bake for 45 minutes, or until potatoes are tender.

Marinated Pork Roast

½ cup (4 fl. oz.) soy sauce
½ cup (4 fl. oz.) dry sherry
2 cloves garlic, minced
1 tablespoon dry mustard
1 teaspoon ginger
1 teaspoon thyme
1 pork roast, 4 to 5 pounds

Combine soy sauce, sherry, garlic, mustard, ginger, and thyme. Place roast in a deep bowl and pour marinade over it. Cover tightly and marinate for 2 to 3 hours at room temperature or overnight in a refrigerator. Turn occasionally.

Preheat oven to 325° F. (165° C.).

Remove meat from marinade and place on a rack in a shallow roasting pan. Roast for 2½ to 3 hours, or until meat thermometer reaches 170° F. (77° C.). Baste occasionally with marinade during the last hour of roasting.

Stir-Fry Ground Pork

1 pound ground pork
2 green bell peppers, thinly sliced
1 cup (6 oz.) celery, sliced
1 large onion, chopped
3 tablespoons cornstarch
¼ cup (2 fl. oz.) water
1 teaspoon salt
¾ cup (6 fl. oz.) water
¼ cup (1¾ oz.) brown sugar
¼ cup (2 fl. oz.) vinegar
3 tablespoons soy sauce
1½ cups (12 oz.) fresh pineapple chunks
3 cups (8 oz.) cooked rice, hot

In a frying pan, sauté ground pork over medium heat until light brown. Drain fat, if necessary, reserving 2 tablespoons. Add green pepper, celery, and onion; sauté for 5 minutes. Meanwhile, in a cup, combine cornstarch and ¼ cup (2 fl. oz.) water, stirring well to dissolve. In a small saucepan, combine salt, ¾ cup (6 fl. oz.) water, brown sugar, vinegar, and soy sauce. Bring to a boil and slowly add cornstarch mixture, stirring until thickened. Pour over pork mixture, add pineapple, cover, and simmer until vegetables are tender-crisp. Serve over rice.

South Pacific Pork Kabobs

¼ cup (2 fl. oz.) soy sauce
¼ cup (2 fl. oz.) water
¼ cup (1½ oz.) green onion, sliced
3 tablespoons sugar
1 tablespoon lemon juice
1 tablespoon fresh ginger root, grated
1 clove garlic, minced
½ teaspoon pepper, coarse ground
¾ pound boneless pork, cut into 1-inch (2½-cm.)
  cubes
3 tablespoons peanut butter
1 teaspoon cornstarch
⅓ cup (2⅔ fl. oz.) milk
⅓ cup (2⅔ fl. oz.) chicken broth
2 tablespoons green onion, chopped
¼ teaspoon garlic salt
dash pepper

In a small bowl, combine soy sauce, water, ¼ cup (1½ oz.) onion, sugar, lemon juice, ginger root, garlic, and pepper. Add pork cubes, tossing to coat. Marinate for 8 hours or overnight in refrigerator.

Prepare barbecue, if used. Thread pork on skewers. Cook on grill over low heat until tender, about 8 to 10 minutes on each side. (Or broil at moderate temperature 3 to 5 inches from heat until tender, about 8 minutes on each side.)

Meanwhile, in a small saucepan, blend peanut butter and cornstarch. Stir in milk, chicken broth, 2 tablespoons onion, garlic salt, and pepper. Cook, stirring constantly, over moderate heat until mixture thickens and bubbles. Cook 1 minute longer. Serve peanut butter sauce with pork.

Pork Balls on Parslied Noodles

1 cup (4 oz.) bread crumbs
¼ cup (2 fl. oz.) milk
1 pound ground pork
1 egg
¼ cup (1½ oz.) onion, chopped
1 teaspoon salt
1 teaspoon lemon juice
¼ teaspoon paprika
⅛ teaspoon nutmeg
4 tablespoons (2 fl. oz.) butter
1 tablespoon all-purpose flour
¼ teaspoon dry mustard
1½ cups (12 fl. oz.) milk
3 to 4 cups (8 oz.) egg noodles
2 tablespoons parsley, chopped

To prepare pork balls, soak bread crumbs in milk for a few minutes. Add ground pork, egg, onion, salt, lemon juice, paprika, and nutmeg; mix well. Shape into 18 to 24 balls. Melt 1 tablespoon butter in 10-inch (25-cm.) skillet. Brown pork balls well on all sides, turning as needed. Cover and cook slowly for about 20 minutes, until pork is cooked. Remove pork balls from skillet; keep warm.

Add 1 tablespoon butter to skillet; melt. Blend in flour and mustard. Add milk; cook until sauce is thickened, stirring constantly. Return pork balls to skillet; heat thoroughly. Cook noodles as directed on package. Drain well. Toss with 2 tablespoons butter, melted, and sprinkle with parsley. Serve pork balls and sauce over noodles.

CONTRIBUTORS

We are grateful to the following individual growers and associations who shared with us their recipes, advice, and suggestions. They have become our friends and we value their excellent contributions.

Almond Beef Hawaiian, California Almond Growers Exchange
Almond Chocolate Soufflé, California Almond Growers Exchange
Almond Paste Bars, Hattie Weststeyn
Almond Pears and Chicken, California Tree Fruit Agreement
Almond Slaw, California Almond Growers Exchange
Almond Tea Cookies, Hattie Weststeyn
Apple and Pork Loin Roast, Norma Brubaker
Apple Buttermilk Bran Muffins, Joan Delfino
Apple Celery Salad, Norma Brubaker
Apricot Brandy Alexander, California Apricot Advisory Board
Apricot Cobbler, Eddie Tufts
Apricot Creams, Eddie Tufts
Apricot Sunshine Breakfast Cake, California Apricot Advisory Board
Artichoke Loaf, Albina Boggiatto
Artichoke Nut Chiffon Cake, Sindone Bellone
Artichoke Pie, Sindone Bellone
Artichoke Quiche, Dolores Tottino
Artichokes and Spaghetti, Albina Boggiatto
Artichoke Sunflower, California Artichoke Advisory Board
Artichoke with Ricotta Mushroom Filling, California Artichoke Advisory Board
Asparagus Frittata, Lillian Mazzanti
Asparagus Sauté, Inez Del Carlo
Asparagus Soup, Lillian Mazzanti

Chicken Liver Pâté, Diamond Walnut Growers
Chili Verde, Sally Shannon
Chili Bean Soup, California Dry Bean Advisory Board
Chilindron, Doris Indart
Chilled Apricot Salad, California Apricot Advisory Board
Chilled Fallbrook Soup, Carolyn Leavens
Chocolate Cookie Sheet Cake, Aileen Carriere
Chris' Cloud Sandwiches, American Egg Advisory Board
Cider Apple Crisp, Nancy Bolster
Clam Chowder, California Milk Advisory Board
Corn and Tomato Chowder, Linda Padilla Macedo
Corn Omelet, Linda Padilla Macedo
Cream of Fresh Pea Soup, California Milk Advisory
    Board
Cream of Rice Soup, Farmers' Rice Cooperative
Creole Steak Strips, Judy Palenske
Crunchy Pear Salad, California Tree Fruit Agreement
Crunchy Rice Salad, Aileen Carriere
Curried Chicken, Foster Farms
Deep-Fried Asparagus, Lillian Mazzanti
Delaware Crackling Bread, California Honey Advisory
    Board
Del Mar Molded Salad, Carolyn Leavens
Dutch Almond Cookies, Hattie Weststeyn
Eggaroni, American Egg Advisory Board
Fiesta Beef, California Beef Council
Flank Steak Roll, Sally Shannon
Fresh Corn Appetizer Dip, Linda Padilla Macedo
Fresh Corn Salad, Linda Padilla Macedo
Fresh Corn Soufflé, Pat Stuhaan
Fresh Peach Cobbler, Ruby Bergman
Fresh Peach Fizz, California Tree Fruit Agreement
Fresh Tomato Pizza, Adele Giovannetti
Fresh Tomato Salsa Appetizer, Evelyn Marquez
Fresh Tomato Sauce and Red Pasta, Adele Giovannetti
Fresh Tomato Summer Salad, Adele Giovannetti
Garden Salad with Poppy Seed Dressing, California
    Fresh Tomato Market Advisory Board

Garlichokes, Albina Boggiatto
Georgia Apple Bars, Geri Hyder
Giant Apple Pancake, Thelma Ford
Glazed Meatballs with Pears, California Tree Fruit
    Agreement
Gold-Strike Punch, American Egg Advisory Board
Golden Glow Chicken, California Honey Advisory Board
Graham Cracker Cream Pie, Jill Martin
Grandma's Pickled Apricots, Eddie Tufts
Green Noodle Tetrazzini, Foster Farms
Ground–Lamb Casserole, Doris Indart
Guacamole Grande, Carolyn Leavens
Hearty Pink Beans, Cleo Schreiner
Honey–Chocolate Freezer Cake, Christine Brandi
Hungryman's Grilled Sandwich, Sunkist Growers,
    Incorporated
Kentucky Fried Corn, Pat Stuhaan
Lace–Edge Breakfast Cakes, Farmers' Rice Cooperative
Lamb and Bean Bake, Doris Indart
Lamb Salad, Doris Indart
Lemon–Fricasseed Chicken, Foster Farms
Lemon Honey Squares, Ann Beekman
Lemon Milk Sherbet, California Milk Advisory Board
Loafer's Peachy French Toast, California Tree Fruit
    Agreement
Marinated Pork Roast, Delores Steiner
Meat Loaf, California Dried Beans Advisory Board
Mexican Corn on the Cob, Pat Stuhaan
Mixed Bean Salad, California Dried Beans Advisory
    Board
Moist Apple Bread, Thelma Ford
Molded Peaches and Cream Dessert, Donna Starn
New England Apple Sauce Loaf Cake, Thelma Ford
Orange Baked–Chicken Appetizers, Foster Farms
Orange Ice, Billie Falkner Israel
Orange Meringue Pie, Darlene Schonauer
Orange Nut Bread, Darlene Schonauer
Orange Pumpkin Custard Pie, Betty Hammill

Roasted Soy Walnuts, Betty Lindeman
Ruby Game Hens, Sherry Mehl
Salinas Bean Bake, Lynn Christierson
San Clemente Curry, Carolyn Leavens
San Juan Cocktail, Carolyn Leavens
Savory Rice, Broccoli and Cheese Bake, Rice Growers
    Association of California
Scalloped Fresh Corn, Linda Padilla Macedo
Sherried Orange Dessert, Darlene Schonauer
Shish Kabob, Doris Indart
Shortribs in Beer, Gertrude Gehrt
Shrimp and Tomatoes with Savory Rice, California Fresh
    Tomato Market Advisory Board
Shrimp Scampi, California Apricot Advisory Board
Skillet Orange Chicken, Sunkist Growers, Incorporated
Skillet Tostada Dinner, Rice Growers Association of
    California
Sole in Almond Shrimp Sauce, California Almond
    Growers Exchange
Something Special Orange Coffee Cake, Billie Falkner
    Israel
Sour Cream Pear Pie, Gerda Faye
South Pacific Pork Kabobs, National Pork Producers
    Council
South Seas Walnut Salad, Diamond Walnut Growers
Spinach Cheese Soufflé, California Milk Advisory Board
Stir-Fry Ground Pork, Barbara Chittenden
Stir-Fry Zucchini and Carrots, California Honey
    Advisory Board
Strawberry Bread, Sherry Mehl
Strawberry Cream Dip, Sherry Mehl
Strawberry Daiquiri, Sherry Mehl
Strawberry Fondue, Sherry Mehl
Strawberry Lemonade, California Strawberry Advisory
    Board
Strawberry Pie, California Strawberry Advisory Board
Strawberries Romanoff, California Strawberry Advisory
    Board
Strawberry Sorbet, Sherry Mehl

Strawberry Thickshakes, California Strawberry
    Advisory Board
Sunny Winter Omelet, American Egg Advisory Board
Swedish Meatballs, Nora Jean Lietz
Sweet–and–Sour Chicken Tidbits, Foster Farms
Sweet–and–Sour Spinach Salad, California Honey
    Advisory Board
Three–Generation Salad, Carolyn Leavens
Tomato Avocado Pita Sandwiches, California Fresh
    Tomato Market Advisory Board
Tomatoes and Peas in Mustard Dill Sauce, California
    Fresh Tomato Market Advisory Board
Tomato Zucchini Parmesan, California Fresh Tomato
    Market Advisory Board
Very Easy Gazpacho, Carolyn Leavens
Walnut Animal Crackers, Diamond Walnut Growers
Walnut Salad Athena, Diamond Walnut Growers
Walnut–Spinach Pie with Mushroom Sauce, Gerda Faye
Walnut Swiss Cheese Tarts, Diamond Walnut Growers
Western Orange–Egg Scramble, Sunkist Growers,
    Incorporated
Whipped Cream with Honey, California Honey Advisory
    Board
World's Easiest Soufflé, American Egg Advisory Board
Yogurt Fruit Salad, California Apricot Advisory Board
Zucchini Quiche in Brown Rice Crust, Rice Growers
    Association of California
Zucchini Walnut Bread, Gerda Faye

INDEX